25th Anniversary Edition

THE

NORTHWEST GOLFER

Oregon Edition

A guide to every golf course

where the public is welcome

in the state of Oregon

By

KiKi Canniff

THE

NORTHWEST GOLFER

Oregon Edition

A guide to every golf course

where the public is welcome

in the state of Oregon

Cover Design

Heather Kibbey - Northwest Publishers Consortium - Lake Oswego, OR - www.NPCBooks.com

Publisher

One More Press – www.OneMorePress.com

ISBN: 978-0-941361-477

TABLE OF CONTENTS

INTRODUCTION

This book describes every golf course in Oregon where the public can play, without purchasing a membership. Besides public courses, it includes all of the region's semi-private courses that provide regularly scheduled times for public play. In all, this book covers 144 golf course locations; some offer more than one course.

Unless you're looking for membership in a private club, this is the only guide an Oregon golfer will ever need. This book is also available in eBook format, so golfers can store it on their cell phone or laptop. That way, no matter where a golfer travels in Oregon, he or she can always find the closest course.

A quick reference line at the beginning of each listing lets you instantly determine if a course is right for your schedule and budget.

How to use The Northwest Golfer

This edition of The Northwest Golfer covers all of Oregon's courses; a second volume provides full details on Washington's courses.

This book begins with a brief introduction, and a map showing how the state has been divided into four regions: Coast, I-5 Corridor, Central and Eastern Oregon. In the book, each region has its own section. The following map shows those four sections.

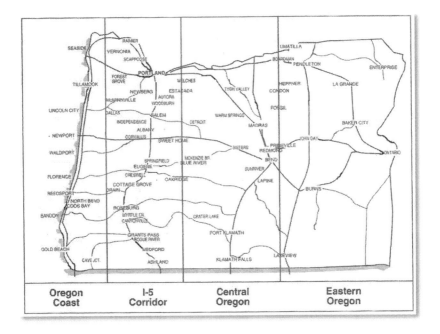

| Oregon Coast | I-5 Corridor | Central Oregon | Eastern Oregon |

Every section begins with a map of the region; every town with a golf course open to the public appears on that map. Listings for all of those cities and their golf courses follow.

What you'll find in each Course Listing

Throughout this book, course listings begin with complete contact information. This is where you'll find the name of the course, its location, website link (if available), and reservation or pro shop phone number.

Right below the course name you'll find that quick reference line highlighting the number of holes available, total yardage from the longest tees, men's par, and price category.

The price category is defined by one to five dollar signs. A single dollar sign calls your attention to a bargain course, two shows it is moderately priced, three denotes a higher-priced course, four is expensive, and five denotes a deluxe or super-expensive golf course.

The actual dollar amounts used to categorize the courses is based on the lowest rate available to all golfers. On an expensive course it could indicate off-season or twilight rates. Prices could be higher during peak schedules.

The exact breakdown is as follows:

$ - Under $15.00

$$ - $15.01 to $30.00

$$$ - $30.01 to $45.00

$$$$ - $45.01 - $75.00

$$$$$ - $75.01-$225.00

Once you have determined that a course fits your needs, read the full listing and you'll learn what the terrain is like, when it is open, whether or not they take reservations, and what makes that particular course special.

You'll find out exactly how much they charge for green fees and rental equipment, whether or not they have discount days or times when everyone can play for reduced fees, the women's par, and if juniors or seniors can play for discounted rates. Unless otherwise noted, junior rates are for those 17 and under; senior rates are for golfers 65 and older.

Facilities are described next. If the course has a putting green, driving range, practice area, or offers lessons, this book lets you know. It will tell you whether you'll find a snack bar, restaurant, lounge, or overnight accommodations too. And, you'll learn if they offer banquet facilities, serve alcohol, or provide help with tournament planning.

At the end of each listing you'll find concise, easy-to-follow directions.

Locating a Favorite Course

To locate all of the golf courses in a particular city quickly, go to the region where that city is located; the cities are then listed alphabetically, and all courses found in or near that city follow.

In the index you will find every course listed by golf course name, allowing you to instantly locate any course you already know by name. The index also includes city page numbers and groupings by cost, course length, and important features.

The author has made every effort to include all of the region's public and semi-private courses, and has worked with the staff at each course to provide accurate information.

The Northwest Golfer has been around since 1987. This edition has been completely updated, and all of the state's new public courses have been added. With this edition the book has been broken into two volumes; one for Oregon and another for Washington.

AN INTRODUCTION TO OREGON'S GOLF COURSES

Oregon is a great place to golf, with its wide variety of terrains, professional course designs and gorgeous mountain, ocean and desert views. All together, Oregon's public and semi-private golf courses with regular public play give golfers 144 different places to play. Some of these courses have more than one golf course, providing golfers with even more opportunities.

The Oregon Coast region includes ocean-side and coastal mountain courses where deer, elk, waterfowl and other wildlife can be seen. This region's natural terrain provides plenty of water hazards, hills, and forests to keep you on your toes. Coastal courses include one of America's toughest golf courses, the only course in the United States where you can rent antique hickory clubs and play with period golf balls, as well as a golf course that has been compared to Pebble Beach and Spyglass Hill.

The I-5 Corridor is where you find Oregon's population center, the state capitol and its biggest city, Portland. So it makes perfect sense that this is also the region with the most public golf courses. These courses are home to some of the toughest holes in the state, and include a haunted golf course as well as one with its own covered bridge. Portland's golfers have nearly three dozen courses from which to choose in and near the city.

These include three multiple course sites; in Portland, Glendoveer and Heron Lakes each offer two 18-hole courses; West Linn's Sandelie Golf Course has both an 18-hole and a 9-hole course.

East of Portland, The Resort at the Mountain has three 9-hole courses and some of the finest greens in the region. South of Portland, at Wilsonville, Charbonneau also offers three 9-hole courses.

In Central Oregon just about every course includes a gorgeous view of snow-capped mountains. This region's courses include plenty of natural hazards and roughs; play around rolling hills, desert sand, ancient lava fields, natural water hazards, canyons and gullies sure to tax your skills. At Sunriver you'll find three 18-hole courses designed by some of golf's best course designers, all at one location. The Pronghorn course has 18 holes; nine designed by Jack Nicklaus and nine designed by Tom Fazio. Central Oregon has seen lots of new courses built in recent years.

Eastern Oregon has high desert golf courses with lots of natural gullies, canyons, water, sagebrush and trees to keep the game interesting. The Big River course in Umatilla will give you a challenging 18 holes and a view of the Columbia River. At Milton-Freewater the course has a 125' change in elevation between the bottom and upper nine, and some fabulous views of the Walla Walla Valley and Blue Mountains. The towering Wallowa Mountains can be seen from Enterprise's Alpine Meadows course; it sits 3756' above sea level.

Golfers in Oregon can play within view of the Pacific Ocean or surrounded by snow capped mountains, tee off on fairways shadowed by thick forests or within view of a clear mountain stream, sink a putt in the high mountain desert or beside a wetland frequented by migrating waterfowl. These are just a few of the magnificent golfing environments you can enjoy while playing in the Beaver State.

The listings on the following pages are sure to make any golfer anxious for a day on the fairways. An avid weekend golfer, someone who plays 1-2 times a week, 40-50 weeks out of the year, could play all of Oregon's 144 courses in just a couple of years, and be qualified to say ... *"I've golfed every course in Oregon!"*

Region One

The Oregon Coast

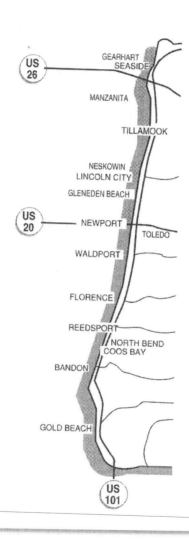

COURSES AT OR NEAR THE OREGON COAST

This region includes the west side of the Oregon Coast Mountains, as well as all the land that lies between those tree-covered mountains and the thundering Pacific Ocean. Included within this region are a golf course said to rival Pebble Beach and Spyglass Hill, one with a green 100 yards from the ocean's edge, another said to be one of the United States' toughest courses, plus lots of golfing fun in the fresh ocean and mountain air.

Elk, deer, wildlife and waterfowl frequent many of these courses; one course even has a visiting flock of sheep. The Chinook Winds Resort and Salishan Lodge are two great places for overnight couples where only one person is interested in golfing; both have lots for a non-golfer to do, so the golfing spouse can get out and enjoy the links.

The following cities at or near the Oregon Coast have golf courses open to the public.

Bandon	Neskowin
Coos Bay	Newport
Florence	North Bend
Gearhart	Reedsport
Gleneden Beach	Seaside
Gold Beach	Tillamook
Lincoln City	Toledo
Manzanita	Waldport

Bandon

Bandon Crossings Golf Course
18 Holes <> Par 71 <> Length 5683 yards <> $$$
87530 Dew Valley Lane - Bandon, OR
541-347-3232
www.bandoncrossings.com

Cited as one of the top ten new courses opened in 2007, Bandon Crossings is a beautiful course, and enjoyable whether you walk or take a motorized cart. Every hole is different, reflecting the land around it, as it follows the contours of ancient sand dunes, streams and woods. Dan Hixson is the designer.

November thru March the rates are $45; during twilight hours it's $35. June thru September you'll pay $75 and $45; April thru May, and in October, 18 holes are $55; during twilight it's $40. Pull carts are $5 and motorized carts are $18 for one golfer or $30 for two. Rental clubs are $20 for 9 holes or $35 for 18.

You'll find a driving range, putting greens, and a practice area. You can arrange for lessons at the pro shop. The driving range has grass tees.

Directions: Located 5 miles south of Bandon Face, on Highway 101.

Bandon Dunes Golf Resort

36 Holes <> Par 72 <> Length 6732 yards <> $$$$$
57744 Round Lake Drive - Bandon, OR
888-345-6008
www.bandondunesgolf.com

Bandon Dunes is advertised as the spirit of Scotland's ancient links situated along Oregon's rugged coast. Four distinctly different courses have been carved out here, in harmony with the surrounding environment. The lies are tight, allowing a player to showcase their skills. Massive dunes and pines, with the roar of the ocean coming from the west, make this a gorgeous place to play.

The first 9 holes opened in 1999; **Bandon Dunes** was designed by David McLay Kidd. The **Pacific Dunes** course debuted in 2001, has natural bunkers, and can be quite windy. **Bandon Trails** opened in 2005 and sits atop a massive sand dune; it an easy-to-walk course. The fourth course, **Old Macdonald**, has fierce bunkers and lots of angles.

Green fees vary depending on the time of year. May thru October resort guests pay $225 to play; the first two weeks in November everyone pays $130. After November 20th, and until the end of January, the rate is $75; in February that increases to $90, in March $120 and it costs $165 during April.

Facilities include a lodge, restaurant and a full service pro shop where you can arrange for lessons and get help with troublesome shots. The restaurant features Pacific

Northwest cuisine and a world-class wine list. A bar and a pub are also on site.

Directions: Located just a few miles off Highway 101, at Bandon.

Bandon Face Rock Golf
9 Holes <> Par 32 <> Length 2,096 yards <> $$
3235 Beach Loop Drive - Bandon, OR
541-329-1927

If you enjoy an ocean-side game of golf, played on Scottish-style bent grass, you'll enjoy the Bandon Face Rock course. The 9th tee is located just 200 yards from the Pacific Ocean.

There has been a golf course here since 1929, when the original course was opened; for many years it was called Bandon Golf Links. Designed by Lee Smith, this course has a 116 slope and a 31.5 course rating. A year-round creek touches 7 holes, making this a challenging little spot, especially when the ocean winds pick up.

This is the only course in the United States to offer the opportunity to play with authentic hickory clubs and real gutta percha balls. At the clubhouse you'll find a collection of 1880's and 1920's hickory clubs for rent. They also offer period-appropriate balls if you want to really test your skills. The Scottish Blackface Sheep that wander around the course add atmosphere to an old-style game.

The Bandon Face Rock course recently re-opened with new bunkers and larger greens. Although it's a relatively flat course, it is among the most challenging 9-hole courses in the Pacific Northwest. This course has five par 4's; the rest are par 3's. Designed to work your short game, the holes have a 150-160 yard average. A second set of tees can be used to play 18 holes. The distance from the women's tees is 1,915 yards.

On Tuesdays they offer a 2-man team rate ($12 each). On Fridays a group of four can play Flogton-style for $50 ($12.50 each); pairs play for $30 ($15 each). The rest of the week, regular green fees are $20.00 for 9 holes, $28.00 to go around twice. They rent clubs, handcarts and motorized carts; two golfers playing 9 holes will pay $14.00 for a cart. Call ahead as this course can be reserved for tournaments and private parties, and on those days the public can't play.

You'll find a clubhouse with an ocean view, a restaurant and lounge with a banquet room, and a full-service pro shop on site. A chipping green, golf lessons, and help with tournament planning are all available. The clubhouse serves a selection of Oregon sandwiches, and can pack golfers a picnic lunch, complete with beer or wine, to enjoy during their game.

Directions: At Bandon take Sea Bird Lane west toward Beach Loop Drive and the course. It is located behind the Best Western Inn at Face Rock; use the hotel's main driveway to enter the golf course.

Coos Bay

Sunset Bay Golf Course
9 Holes <> Par 36 <> Length 3020 yards <> $
11001 Cape Arago Hwy. - Coos Bay, OR
541-888-9301
www.sunsetbaygolf.com

Nearly every hole at Sunset Bay has a water hazard or two. This not only keeps the game interesting, but also creates a beautiful setting. The course sits in a valley and has several elevated greens and tees. Bordered by dense forest, it is fairly easy to walk. Designed by John Zoller, it opened in 1969.

Big creeks touch eight of Sunset Bay's nine holes; and there are two feeder ponds to boot. A double set of tees makes 18 more enjoyable.

The challenging dogleg on the 8th hole winds thru cedar stumps on its 450 yard journey to the green. The white/red tees have a total distance of 2609 yards.

Weekday green fees are $15 for 9 or $25 for 18; on the weekend you'll pay $18 and $28. Clubs rent for $9-14, pull carts are $3, and motorized carts are $16 for 9 holes or $30 for 18.

Directions: Located 3 miles east of the Bay Bridge.

Watson Ranch Golf

18 Holes <> Par 72 <> Length 6402 yards <> $$
93884 Coos Sumner Lane - Coos Bay, OR
541-267-7257
www.watsonranchgolf.com

This was the old Coos Country Club. The original nine holes were designed by Chandler Egan and opened in 1923; the back nine was designed by Bill Robinson and opened in 1998.

In 2006 this course was purchased by Watson Ranch Development, and opened to the public.

Green fees during the summer are $25 for 9 holes or $40 for 18. During the winter you'll pay $20-30. Juniors, age 15 and younger, can play 9 holes for $13 year round; 18 holes will cost them $25.

You'll find a driving range, chipping area and two practice putting greens. Lessons are available, and they offer golf clinics for juniors.

RV travelers purchasing one 18-hole round of golf, with a cart, will get one free overnight parking space if they arrive early enough.

Directions: Located 5 miles south of Coos Bay, via Highway 101.

Florence

Ocean Dunes Golf Links

18 Holes <> Par 71 <> Length 5683 yards <> $$
3345 Munsel Lake Road - Florence, OR
800-468-4833
www.oceandunesgolf.com

Ocean Dunes Golf Links is built on rolling sand dunes and bordered by natural rhododendron, beach grass and native plants; the slope is 124 and the ratings 68.5 for men and 69.5 for women. The original 9 holes were built in 1962; the second in 1989.

Narrow fairways, with small greens guarded by bunkers, and a rough consisting of dunes, sea grasses and gorse make it quite challenging. Open year round, reservations are available two weeks in advance. The back nine offers a panoramic view of the Florence area, and the women's par is 72 for a total distance of 4881 yards.

Green fees are $25 for 9 holes or $48 for 18 May thru October; $20 and $33 the balance of the year. Summer twilight rates begin at 2pm and are $25 whether you play 9 or 18. Juniors, 17 and younger, can play the course for $10 any time of the year. Clubs and handcarts are available for rental; motorized carts rent for $18-28.

Facilities include a snack bar offering beer and wine, plus a pro shop and driving range. Lessons can be arranged, and they can provide help with tournaments too.

Directions: Located northeast of Florence; follow Spruce Street toward 18th Street and turn left onto Highway 126. Follow this for .8 mile and turn left onto North Fork Suislaw Road; turn left onto Munsel Lake Road and follow .5 mile to the course.

Sandpines Golf Resort
18 Holes <> Par 72 <> Length 7190 yards <> $$$$
1201 35th Street - Florence, OR
541-997-1940 - Reservations Advised
www.sandpines.com

This Rees Jones designed course has been compared to Pebble Beach and Spyglass Hill. Giant sand dunes, deep man-made lakes, Monterey pines and cypress trees make it both challenging and beautiful.

The slope ranges from 111 to 129 for men with course ratings of 65.8 to 74. The women's slope is 122-131, and 70.4 to 75.2. Four sets of tees are available; the distance ranges from 5323 yards from the front tees to 7190 from the tournament tees. Spring and summer hours are 7am to dusk; in the fall and winter they open up at 8am.

You'll pay $79 to play 18 holes at Sandpines June thru September, every day of the week. In May and October it's $10 cheaper when you play during the week. In April you pay $69 all week long; November thru March it's only $49. Juniors, age 9-17, can play for reduced rates. Rental clubs are available; they rent motorized carts for $16 per rider.

Facilities include the Tavolo Restaurant and Lounge, open Wednesday thru Sunday from 11:30am to 5pm. Sandpines also has a full-service pro shop where you can get help with tournaments and golf lessons, and a driving range. The driving range charges $5 for a bucket of balls.

Directions: Located at the north end of town.

Gearhart

Gearhart Golf Links
18 Holes <> Par 72 <> Length 6218 yards <> $$
1157 N. Marion - Gearhart, OR
(503) 738-3538
www.gearhartgolflinks.com

Established in 1892, Gearhart Golf Links is the oldest golf course in the Pacific Northwest, and began with just three sandy holes. The other 6 holes were opened in 1901, and the second 9 in 1913. A redesign by Chandler Egan, and other changes made between 1926 and 1935, resulted in the current layout.

Built on softly rolling dunes, this links-style course is situated just off the Pacific Ocean, and is a classic example of early links-style golf. The terrain is rugged and windswept; the slope is 114 and the course rating

68.7. Open year round, from dawn to dusk, they have five sets of tees, ranging from 5154 to 5922 yards.

Green fees Monday thru Thursday are $65, the rest of the week you'll pay $75. At 1pm rates drop to $50, at 3pm $35, and at 5pm $25. A child younger than 13 plays for free with a paying adult, those 13-18 pay $15, and students 19-24 pay $35. Motorized carts rent for $15 per player; $10 after twilight.

This course has a beautiful clubhouse, and a McMenamins Pub overlooking the greens. Banquet facilities, and a full-service pro shop offering lessons and help with tournament planning, are also available.

Directions: Leave Highway 101 in Gearhart and head west to Marion Avenue.

The Highlands Golf Club
9 Holes <> Par 30 <> Length 1852 yards <> $
33260 Highlands Lane - Gearhart, OR
(503) 738-5248
www.highlandsgolfgearhart.com

The ocean view is great at this year-round course, it's suitable for players of all ability levels, and the terrain is one of gently rolling hills. Opened in 1986, the total distance from the white tees is 1552 yards. This course can be played in less than two hours.

For best rates buy a 10-round pass, at $99 you're playing 9 holes for less than $10 a game, or stop in for twilight golf when the rates are $16 for 18 holes. All others pay $15-20 to play. No motorized carts are permitted on the course. They have a large pro shop and can help with tournament planning and lessons. Beer and wine are served on the patio, along with sandwiches and snacks.

Directions: Take the Del Ray Beach exit off Highway 101 and follow the signs; the course road is just west of the highway on the left.

Gleneden Beach

Salishan Golf Links
18 Holes <> Par 72 <> Length 6439 yards <> $$$$
Salishan Lodge - Gleneden Beach, OR
541-764-3632 - Reservations Required
www.salishan.com/golf

Salishan Lodge is a terrific place for a golfing vacation with its spectacular views and old-growth timber. This Scottish-style course is beautifully laid out and is open year round. Built in 1965, the original designers were Fred Federspiel and John Gray; it was later redesigned by Peter Jacobsen. The slope is 128 for a rating of 72.1, and the back nine has spectacular ocean views. Three sets of tees are available.

Memorial Day weekend thru September, green fees are $49-69 for 9 holes and $79-119 for 18, depending on the time of day you play. Green fees are lower off-season, and lodge guests play at discounted rates. Clubs, handcarts and motorized carts are available for rental.

You'll find resort facilities that include a full-service spa, indoor tennis courts, a pool and fitness center, a first class restaurant, a fully-stocked pro shop, putting course and driving range. They can provide help with tournaments and offer lessons.

Directions: Salishan is located just south of Lincoln City on Highway 101.

Gold Beach

Cedar Bend Golf Course
9 Holes <> Par 36 <> Length 3000 yards <> $
34391 Squaw Valley Road - Gold Beach, OR
541-247-6911 - Reservations Advised
www.cedarbendgolf.com

Built in 1969, this year-round course has four sets of tees and two flags on each green. Designed by John Zoller, the slope is 115 and the rating 67.6. Cedar Bend is flat, scenic and surrounded by trees. Water affects most holes, and the women's tees have a total distance of 2605 yards. Deer and elk frequent this course.

Green fees are $20 for 9 holes, or $28 for 18, seven days a week. On weekdays juniors can play for $5-10 depending on their age, and seniors play for $14. After 3:30pm Monday thru Wednesday everyone can take advantage of the Twilight Special; the rate is $15 to play all the way to 8pm. You can rent clubs for $5-7, handcarts are $2, and motorized carts $12-18. The total distance for 18 holes is 5231-6288 yards, depending on which tees you play from.

Facilities include a lounge with a seasonal liquor license plus a snack bar, full service pro shop, and driving range. The driving range has mat tees and charges $2.50 for a small bucket of balls or $5 for a large one. Tournament planning help is available at the pro shop.

Directions: Located 12 miles north of Gold Beach

Lincoln City

Chinook Winds Golf Resort
18 Holes <> Par 68 <> Length 4639 yards <> $$
3245 NE 50th Street - Lincoln City, OR
541-994-8442 - Reservations Advised
www.chinookwindscasino.com

This course is located just north of the Chinook Winds Casino complex, right off Highway 101, and is said to be one of the toughest courses in the U.S.. The red tees have a total distance of 3972 yards for a par of 65.

Green fees are $30 for 9 holes or $40 for 18 when you're walking the course. With a cart those fees will be $40 and $55. Seniors receive a 15% discount and juniors can play 9 holes for $10 or 18 for $20.

During the Twilight Special, 3pm to 6pm daily during the summer, you can play 9 holes for $24 when you walk; $30 gets you a cart too. From 6pm to sundown everyone can walk and golf for $19 or take a cart along for a total of $29.

They have a High Definition Golf Simulator upstairs over the pro shop, a bar and grill and of course, a casino.

Directions: Located near the north end of Lincoln City; follow the casino signs.

Manzanita

Manzanita Golf Course
9 Holes <> Par 32 <> Length 2192 yards <> $$
908 Lakeview Drive - Manzanita, OR
503-368-5744 - Reservations Suggested

Manzanita is a wonderful little ocean-side village with a well-groomed year-round golf course. Designed by Ted Erickson, it opened in 1987. This course offers tree-lined fairways, easy walking, and a pleasant game on a beautiful hillside. On the 5th hole there's a 60 foot drop to the fairway below. The slope is 97 to 102, and the ratings 61.8 for men and 63.2 for women. The second set of tees has a total distance of 2100 yards.

Green fees are $18 for 9 holes or $30 for 18. You can rent clubs for $8 and pull carts for $2. They have a 10-stall driving range and a full-service pro shop. The driving range is open May through September.

Directions: Leave Highway 101 at Manzanita, follow Laneda Avenue to Carmel, and turn left to the course.

Neskowin

Neskowin Marsh Golf Course
9 Holes <> Par 35 <> Length 2591 yards <> $
48405 Hawk Street - Neskowin, OR
503-392-3377 - Reservations Advised

This course was built in 1932 and is one of the oldest along the coast; it floods completely during the winter. Closed November thru April, the flooding is what makes it lush and green all summer long. This is an easy-to-walk flat course where a creek comes into play on half the greens; it crosses the 5th hole twice. The view is spectacular; the slope 110 and the course rating 33.8.

At Neskowin Marsh you'll pay $17.50 to play 9 holes; off season it drops to $12.50, and 18 holes will cost you $20-30 depending on the time of year. Gas carts rent for $10 per 9 holes; handcarts are $2, and clubs $5. Facilities include a snack bar serving beer, and a BBQ facility, plus a pro shop where lessons can be arranged.

Directions: Leave Highway 101 at Neskowin, drive past the rest area and turn right.

Newport

Agate Beach Golf Course
9 Holes <> Par 36 <> Length 2905 yards <> $$
4100 N Coast Hwy. - Newport, OR
541-265-7331
www.agatebeachgolf.net

The Agate Beach Golf Course was built in 1931. It is open year round, fairly level with a slightly rolling terrain, and easy to walk. Surrounded by forests, they keep it well manicured and provide excellent putting surfaces. They are open daily between 7:30am and dusk.

Agate Beach has five par 5's, five 3's and ten 4's. The greens are kept well manicured; the slope is 109, and the ratings 65.8 for men, 68.7 for women. The total distance from the ladies' tees is 2669 yards for a par of 38.

Green fees are $18 for 9 holes or $36 for 18. Clubs rent for $6-10, handcarts $2-4, and motorized carts are $14 per 9 holes. On the driving range you'll pay $3 for 30 balls or $6 for 60.

Facilities include a coffee shop with a hearty menu plus beer and wine, a full-service pro shop, and a driving range. The range is for irons and offers grass tees; it closes at 6pm. Lessons are available.

Directions: Agate Beach is located at the north end of Newport, on Highway 101's east side.

North Bend

Kentuck Golf & Country Club
18 Holes <> Par 70 <> Length 5393 yards <> $$
675 Golf Course Lane - North Bend, OR
541-756-4464

This is the most southern 18-hole course along the Oregon coast, and it's open year round. Designed by Don Houston and Wallace Wickett, the terrain is flat, the greens are small, and the fairways are surrounded by woods. Built in 1965, the slope is 99 for a rating of 65.5. The total distance from the ladies tees is 4469 yards. There's a water hazard in the center of the 17th fairway, giving this 392 yard par 4 a bit of difficulty.

Green fees during the week are $16, and on weekends you'll pay $18. At the clubhouse you get a great view across Coos Bay and North Bend. Facilities include a putting green, practice bunker and chipping area, and they rent clubs and pull carts.

Directions: Located 3 miles east of the Bay Bridge. Leave US 101 at North Bend on East Bay Drive, and after 2.6 miles turn right onto East Bay Road.

Reedsport

Forest Hills Country Club
27 Holes <> Par 36 <> Length 3086 yards <> $$
1 Country Club Drive - Reedsport, OR
541-271-2626 - Reservations Advised
www.golfreedsport.com

Forest Hills is relatively flat, has some hills, and is surrounded by woods. Open 8am to dusk May thru September during the week, they open at 7am on summer weekends. Winter hours are 8am to dusk Tuesday thru Sunday; they open at 10am on Mondays.

This course is has lots of mature fir and alders, and some water. You'll find four sets of tees; the women's par is 37 for a total distance of 2766 yards.

Weekday green fees are $18 for 9 holes, $30 for 18, or you can play all day for $37. If you're active military you can play 9 for $13.50, $18 for $22.50 or pay $29.50 to play all day. Power carts are $14 and $25, pull carts $3-5, and clubs are a flat $10.

They have a restaurant and lounge, pro shop and driving range; at the range you'll pay $3-5 for a bucket of balls.

Directions: You'll find signs on Highway 101, in Reedsport, directing you to this course.

Seaside

Seaside Golf Club
9 Holes <> Par 35 <> Length 2,623 yards <> $
451 Avenue U - Seaside OR
503-738-5261 - No reservations

This course was built in 1921 and is open year round, weather permitting, sunup to sundown. It is situated on the site of the old Ben Holiday house with its historic race track. Designed by H. Chandler Egan, the second green sits just 100 yards from the Pacific Ocean.

THE NORTHWEST GOLFER: OREGON EDITION

The view is pretty, the terrain flat, and you can hear the ocean from a few tees. Every hole has a Necanicum River view and the course crosses the river twice.

The slope is 104 and the ratings 62.9 for men and 65.0 for women. From the red tees the total distance is 2,526 yards.

Punch cards and yearly passes provide the best bargains at Seaside; the punch cards are $275 which give you 25 9-hole games for $11 each, annual passes are $575 for singles and $775 for couples.

Everyone else pays $15 to play 9 holes on weekdays, $28 for 18. On weekends and holidays it'll cost you $17 and $32. On weekdays, anyone older than 65 or younger than 14 can get a $2 discount.

Clubs can be rented for $7-12, handcarts $3-5, and motorized carts $16-30. Golfers with their own cart pay $5-10 to bring them on the trail.

They have a restaurant, open only during the summer between 8am and 3pm Tuesday thru Sunday, plus a pro shop, banquet facilities and a putting green. The covered driving range offers both mat and grass tees.

Directions: The Seaside Golf Club is located at the south end of town.

Tillamook

Alderbrook Golf Course
18 Holes <> Par 69 <> Length 5965 yards <> $
7300 Alderbrook Road - Tillamook, OR
503-842-6413
www.AlderbrookGolfCourse.com

Alderbrook was started in 1924 and offers a great view of Tillamook Bay and the surrounding tree-covered mountains. Its terrain is fairly level with one hill affecting two holes; the 15th hole has a 25% uphill drive for a par three. The view from the top of the 16th hole is gorgeous, and the front nine was recently renovated.

Open year round, reservations are not required. The slope is 103 to 105, and the ratings 66.8 for men or 68.9 for women. From the second set of tees the distance is 5272 yards for a par of 71.

If you play the front 9 at Alderbrook the green fees are $30; the back 9 can be played for $15. There are two ways to play 18 holes; you can play the front 9 twice for $60 or the front and back nines for $45. Junior rates are $7 for the front 9 or $15 to play the full course. They rent clubs and carts at the pro shop. Clubs rent for $10 and up, carts are $20-30 for 2 golfers or $10-15 for one. There's a $5 trail fee if you bring your own cart, and pull carts can be rented for $3-5.

They have a restaurant overlooking the course with a full-service bar; Koko's is open from 11am to 9pm and has a wonderful menu. Banquet facilities are available. They also have a full-service pro shop and private locker rooms for both men and women, with showers. You can get help with tournament planning and lessons at the pro shop.

Directions: Head north on Highway 101, go past the cheese factory and turn right on Alderbrook Road. From there it is about 2 miles.

Bay Breeze Golf Range
9 Holes <> Par 31 <> Length 1061 yards <> $
2325 Latimer Road - Tillamook, OR
503-842-1166 - Reservations Available

Bay Breeze offers plush bent grass greens plus plenty of water hazards and sand traps. The longest hole is 140 yards and the shortest 75, so it's a good place to use your irons. Built in 1994, it was designed by Mike Lehman. Open February thru October, the total distance from the forward tees is 853 yards. The course slope is 113 for a 30.0 rating.

Green fees are just $6 for 9 holes, $10 for 18, all week long. Clubs rent for $3 and handcarts are $1. Motorized carts are not available. Facilities include chipping and putting greens, a covered, lighted driving range plus a putter's stage, lunch bar, and full-service pro shop. You can get help with tournament planning and lessons.

Directions: Follow Highway 101 to the Tillamook Cheese Factory and turn right on Latimer Road.

Toledo

Olalla Valley Golf
9 Holes <> Par 36 <> Length 2920 yards <> $$
1022 Olalla Road - Toledo, OR
541-336-2121 - Reservations Advised

The Olalla Valley course is 7 miles inland and a good place to go when fog socks in the coastal towns. Open year round, it's challenging, hilly, and has enough water to keep you on your toes. It's a nice course to walk during the week.

The 8th green is heart-shaped, and the women's par is 37 for a total distance of 2587 yards. The designer is Vernon Warren; the course has a slope of 127 and a 36.4 rating.

Green fees are the same seven days a week, $18 for 9 holes or $32 for 18. Seniors play for $16 and $28 and juniors $12 and $20. Clubs rent for $7 and $9, pull carts $2 per 9 holes, and motorized carts are $16 and $28.

You'll find a small pro shop, putting green, chipping area, banquet facilities, and a restaurant that serves beer and wine. You can also get help with tournament planning.

Directions: Olalla Valley Golf is located about a mile off Highway 20, near Toledo.

Waldport

Crestview Hills Golf

9 Holes <> Par 36 <> Length 3062 yards <> $$
1680 Crestline Drive - Waldport, OR
541-563-3020
www.crestviewgolfclub.com

You'll get a view of the ocean from Crestview's 8th hole, and the 5th hole is one of the prettiest on the coast. This course first opened in 1969 and was designed by Willard Hall. It has fairly small, but well-manicured greens, a hilly terrain, and a family-friendly atmosphere. The slope is 114 and the course rating 34.8. From the middle tees the total distance is 2856 yards; it's 2634 from the forward tees.

During the summer this course is open at 7am and in the winter 8am. Green fees are $20 for 9 holes or $35 for 18 seven days a week; a cart adds $5 per person per 9 holes. Juniors can play 9 holes for $16 or 18 for $30. Clubs rent for $6 and $9 and pull carts $2 and $3. During the winter everyone plays for reduced rates.

They have a full-service pro shop, driving range, and a seasonal cafe. At the driving range you get a bucket of balls for $3. The parking lot has sufficient space for RV day-parking while you play.

Directions: Take Highway 101 south of Waldport 1 mile to Range Drive and head east 1 mile to the course.

Region Two

The Oregon I-5 Corridor

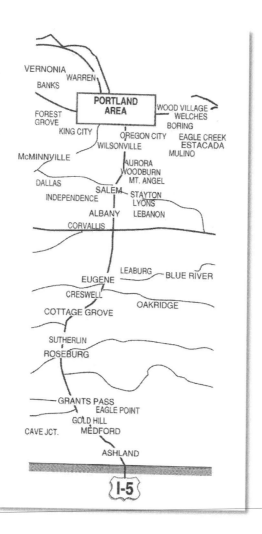

COURSES IN AND NEAR OREGON'S I-5 CORRIDOR

Many of the state's toughest holes are found in this region. Tokatee at Blue River, Emerald Valley at Creswell, the Eagle Creek Golf Course, and Eugene's Laurelwood Golf Course all have holes that have been rated among the most difficult in the state.

Within a 30 minute drive of downtown Portland you'll find nearly three dozen golf courses. Mountain views abound, there's a covered bridge on the Ranch Hills course at Mulino, and McMinnville's Bayou Golf Course is rumored to be haunted.

The following cities in Oregon's I-5 Corridor have golf courses. Cities in the Portland Area are Beaverton, Clackamas, Cornelius, Gladstone, Gresham, Hillsboro, Lake Oswego, Portland, Tigard and West Linn.

Albany
Ashland
Aurora
Banks
Beaverton
Blue River
Boring
Cave Junction
Clackamas
Cornelius
Corvallis
Cottage Grove
Creswell

Dallas
Eagle Creek
Eagle Point
Estacada
Eugene
Forest Grove
Gladstone
Gold Hill
Grants Pass
Gresham
Hillsboro
Independence
King City

Lake Oswego
Leaburg
Lebanon
Lyons
Medford
McMinnville
Mt. Angel
Mulino
Oakridge
Oregon City
Portland
Portland Area

Roseburg
Salem
Stayton
Sutherlin
Tigard
Vernonia
Warren
Welches
West Linn
Wilsonville
Wood Village
Woodburn

Albany

Spring Hill Country Club Golf Course
18 Holes <> Par 72 <> Length 6502 yards <> $$
155 NW Country Club Lane - Albany, OR
541-926-6059 - Reservations Available
www.springhillcc.com

A dry winter course, the course nines were reversed in 2000 following renovations. The slope is 129 and the course rating 71.7.

Summer green fees are $25 for 9 holes or $50 for 18 on weekends, $20 and $40 on weekdays. Twilight rates start 3 hours prior to sunset and are a flat $25. Juniors can play all week long for $10 and $20. Power carts rent for

$14 and $28 and pull carts are $2-3. In the winter green fees drop to $15 and $30.

Facilities include a clubhouse with a restaurant and banquet facilities, a pro shop, driving range and fitness center. Lessons and help with tournament planning are available. At the driving range you'll pay $3-7 for a bucket of balls.

Directions: Follow US Highway 20 west to Springhill Drive and follow the golf course signs.

Ashland

Oak Knoll Golf Course
9 Holes <> Par 36 <> Length 3029 yards <> $
3070 Highway 66 - Ashland, OR
541-482-4311 - Reservations Required
www.oakknollgolf.org

There has been a course here since the 1920's. Oak Knoll provides beautiful mountain views and is open year round. The terrain is hilly and the fairways are lined with trees; the greens are small and well-maintained. Oak Knoll's slope is 114 and the ratings 69.2 for men, 70.5 for women. A second set of tees is available for playing 18 holes. The total yardage from the women's tees is 2671 for a par of 38.

During the week you can play 9 holes for $16 or 18 holes for $24.00; off season you'll pay $2 less. Clubs rent for $12, handcarts $3, and motorized carts are $13 per 9 holes.

They have a restaurant and lounge with a liquor license and banquet facilities, plus a full-service pro shop and practice putting and chipping greens. At the driving range you'll find both grass and mat tees. Lessons, and help with tournament planning, are available.

Directions: This course is located less than a mile off of I-5; take Highway 66 toward Klamath Falls.

Aurora

Langdon Farms Golf Club
18 Holes <> Par 71 <> Length 6950 yards <> $$
24377 NE Airport Road - Aurora, OR
503-678-4653 - Reservations Advised
www.langdonfarms.com

Langdon Farms opened in 1995, and was designed by John Fought and Bob Cupp. The slope is 125 and the rating 71.8. Open year round, from sunup to sundown, this easy-to-walk championship course offers large bent grass tees and a public resort atmosphere.

Located in a farming community, the clubhouse is housed in a big red barn. In 2010 Golfweek Magazine rated this course as one of the ten best to play in Oregon.

Green fees include the use of a motorized cart and vary depending on the season and time of day. Early players pay $44-49, come after 8:15am and you'll pay $59; rates drop again at 11am to $44, at 3:15 you'll pay $34 and at 5:45 $19. Farm card holders pay $34-$39 during the week; after 4pm those rates drop to $29 per player, at 5:30 it drops again to $15.

Facilities include a restaurant and lounge with a liquor license, a patio party area, a full-service pro shop, 3-hole grass putting course, and an 8,000-square-foot practice facility. Known as The Stables, it has 30 lighted bays with turf mats. The range is open until 9pm in the summer but closes an hour earlier the rest of the year.

At the practice range a bucket of balls is $2 for 25 balls, $5 for 65, or $9 for 120. You can get help with tournament planning and golf lessons at the pro shop; they also hold junior golf camps.

Directions: Leave I-5 northbound at exit 282, just south of Wilsonville; head east a quarter mile and turn right onto Airport Road. Follow this road to the golf course. Traveling southbound take exit 282B towards Charbonneau District, turn left on Miley Road, go over the overpass and turn right onto NE Airport Road.

Aumsville

Santiam Golf Club
18 Holes <> Par 72 <> Length 6392 yards <> $$
8724 Golf Club Road SE - Aumsville, OR
503-767-4653 or 503-769-3485
www.santiamgolfclub.com

Built in 1958, the Santiam Golf Club course is flat and open year round. This course was made a reality by seven men from the towns of Sublimity, Aumsville and Stayton. The greens are kept in excellent shape and natural hazards include trees, sand bunkers, a creek and lake. The slope is 123 and the ratings 69.9 for men, 72.2 for women. There are three tees for every hole.

Green fees during the week are $21 for 9 holes or $36 for 18; at noon twilight rates begin and those fees drop to $16 and $26. On weekends and holidays you'll pay $24 and $41; twilight weekend rates are $19 and $35. Juniors can golf for $13 and $21 all week long; twilight rates are $11 and $16. Anyone can buy a punch card for $210 which make 12 nine-hole rounds of golf just $17.50 a game. Carts rent for $14 and $24; after twilight it's $12 and $20. Clubs rent for $10 and $15, pull carts are $4, and trail fees for those bringing their own cart are $10 a day.

They have a restaurant and lounge with a liquor license, plus banquet facilities, a driving range, and a full-service pro shop. At the driving range you'll pay $3 for a bucket of balls. They can also help you with tournament planning and arrange for lessons.

Directions: Leave Oregon Highway 22 heading toward Aumsville and drive 3.8 miles; located at 8724 Golf Club Road SE.

Banks

Quail Valley Golf Course
18 Holes <> Par 72 <> Length 6628 yards <> $$
12565 NW Aerts Road - Banks, OR
503-324-4444
www.qualivalleygolf.com

Designed by John Zoller, Quail Valley opened in 1993. It's a links-style course, flat with hills, and water comes into play on nearly half the holes. You'll find four sets of tees which vary from 5519 yards to 6628. The slope ranges from 114 to 122 and the ratings 68.9 to 71.6. Open year round, hours are 8am to dusk in season; they don't open until 9am in the winter.

Monday thru Thursday green fees are $18 for 9 holes or $35 for 18; get on the course before 9am and you'll pay $16 and $29. On Fridays they charge $19 and $36; early birds pay $17 and $32. Weekend and holiday rates are $20 per 9 holes. During the week seniors, those age 62 and older, pay $26 for 18 holes. Juniors, those 17 and younger, play for half price. Clubs rent for $16, handcarts are $3, and motorized carts $14 per 9 holes.

Facilities include a restaurant and lounge where you'll find cold beer and wine, a full-service pro shop and a driving range. At the range they offer grass tees and you get a bucket of balls for $3 to $7, depending on how many you need. Lessons and help with tournament planning are available.

Directions: Leave Highway 26 at the Banks/Tillamook exit, the course is 1.8 miles down this road.

Blue River

Tokatee Golf Club
18 Holes <> Par 72 <> Length 6806 yards <> $$
54947 McKenzie Hwy. - Blue River, OR
541-822-3220 - Reservations Advised
www.tokatee.com

Tokatee has been ranked among America's top public courses, and its location is one of the prettiest in Oregon. The snow-capped peaks of Three Sisters present a beautiful backdrop for this lake-dotted course. It was designed by Ted Robinson and opened in 1966. The total yardage ranges from 5018 to 6806 yards; the slope is 114-128 and the ratings 68.3-75.5. The terrain is generally flat with some rolling hills, and you'll find three tees per hole. They open around the middle of February and close in mid-November.

Green fees are $24 for 9 holes or $42 for 18 until 12:30pm when they drop to $22 and $35. After 2pm they drop again to $18 and $30. College students can play off-season for $12 and $22. Juniors, those under age 18, can play for $5 year round. Motorized carts rent for $18 and $30. The trail fee, if you bring your own cart, is $14.

Facilities include a restaurant offering beer and wine, plus a banquet room, full-service pro shop and driving range. Lessons and help with tournament planning are available. They have chipping and putting greens as well as a driving range with grass tees.

Directions: Located 6 miles east of Blue River along Highway 126.

Boring

Greenlea Golf Course
9 Holes <> Par 31 <> Length 1657 yards <> $
26736 SE Kelso Road - Boring, OR
503-663-3934
www.greenleagolfcourse.com

Considering its proximity to Portland, this course is a real bargain. Open from mid-February thru October, weekday hours are 8am to 7pm; on weekends and holidays they open an hour earlier. This land was once a nursery and looks like a large park. You'll find five par 3's and four par 4's; the blue tees have a total distance of 1657 yards, the white tees 1534 yards.

Greenlea is well kept and has good drainage. You'll find very few hills here, nothing steep, and it's easy to walk. They have a limited pro shop where you'll find snacks and cold drinks.

During the week 9 holes will cost you $10; on weekends and holidays you'll pay $13. Seniors, those over age 60, can play during the week for $9; juniors play for $7. Clubs can be rented for $5 and handcarts $3. They have one electric cart, reserved for a disabled golfer, that rents for $10; all others must walk the course.

Directions: Located 1.5 miles south of Boring, half mile west of the Mountain View course. Leave Highway 26 on SE Kelso Road and drive 3.5 miles to the golf course.

Mountain View Golf
18 Holes <> Par 71 <> Length 6200 yards <> $
27195 SE Kelso Road - Boring, OR
503-663-4869 - Reservations Recommended

Mountain View is open year round. Built in 1964, it has a beautiful view of Mt. Hood, Mt. Adams and Mount St. Helens. The rolling terrain presents a challenge to most golfers, and the 12th hole has a 200 foot vertical drop. From the championship tees the slope is 119 and the rating 68.7. For women, the slope is 113 and rating 69.2; the total distance is 5202 yards for a par of 71. There is a third set of tees with a distance of 5548 yards.

Green fees during the week are $15 for 9 holes and $20 for 18, but juniors and seniors qualify for a discount. Everybody pays $25 and $30 on weekends and holidays. Clubs rent for $5 per 9 holes and handcarts are $2. Motorized carts are $10 per rider during the week, $15 per rider on weekends and holidays.

Amenities include a pro shop, restaurant and lounge, banquet facilities, chipping and putting greens, and a driving range with mat tees. Lessons are available.

Directions: Located 1 mile south of Boring; leave Highway 212 at Boring and follow the signs.

Cave Junction

Illinois Valley Golf Club
9 Holes <> Par 36 <> Length 3051 yards <> $
25320 Redwood Hwy. - Cave Junction, OR
541-592-3151 - Reservations Advised

You'll find two tees, making this flat semi-private 9-hole course an interesting 18. The slope for men is 121 for a rating of 69.2, for women it's 124 and 71.5. The total distance from the ladies' tees is 2732 yards.

Creeks run through this course, and the pond seems to attract a lot golf balls; the fairways are narrow and the greens are small. Located in the beautiful Illinois Valley, this course is open year round from dawn to dusk. Designed by Bob and Robert Baldock, it first opened in 1976.

Green fees are $12 for 9 holes, $18 for 18, all week long. Junior and senior discounts are available. Clubs rent for $5, handcarts $2, and motorized carts $11 per 9 holes. You can get help with tournament planning and arrange for lessons at the pro shop.

They have chipping and putting greens, a driving range with grass tees, and a snack bar where you can get cold beer and wine.

Directions: Located 1.1 miles north of Cave Junction, at the junction of Highway 199N and Laurel Road.

Corvallis

Golf City
9 Holes <> Par 28 <> Length 801 yards <> $
2115 Highway 20 - Corvallis, OR
541-753-6213
www.golfcitypar3.com

Golf City is flat and a great place for beginners. The 9th hole is one of the shortest known par 4's around, measuring just 85 yards. The other 8 holes are all par 3's on this year-round course. Built in 1977, the designer was Ed Burns; it has winter rye fairways and bent grass greens.

Green fees are $8 seven days a week. Juniors, 12 and younger, as well as seniors, age 60 and over, can play 9 holes before noon for $5.75. Golf clubs can be borrowed for free. Facilities include a pub with a full menu and cold beer, a full-service pro shop, and an 18-hole miniature golf course known as Beaver Falls. At the miniature golf course kids 12 and younger play for $3.50, everyone else pays $5.

Directions: Located on US 26 near NE Circle Blvd.

Marysville Golf Course

9 Holes <> Par 36 <> Length 3171 yards <> $$
2020 SW Allen Street - Corvallis, OR
541-753-3421
www.marysvillegolf.net

Marysville is a family-owned course that was designed by Fred Federspiel and built in 1958. It is relatively flat, the fairways are straight and easy to walk, and the fairways and greens are bent grass. This course is open year round; the slope is 114 and the course rating 34.5. The red tees have a total distance of 2681 yards, and the white 3025.

Green fees at Marysville are $18 for 9 holes or $26 for 18 seven days a week. Seniors play for $16 and $24; juniors age 8-17 for $10 and $15, and students age 18-23 pay $14 and $22. On non-holiday Mondays everyone saves $2. You can rent golf clubs for $4 and pull carts for $3; some motorized carts are available.

Facilities include a putting green, covered driving range, and a minimal pro shop where you'll find light snacks and cold beer.

Directions: Leave Highway 99 at the Corvallis Avery Park exit. Turn left on Allen Street; the course is at the end of the road.

Trysting Tree Golf Club
18 Holes <> Par 72 <> Length 7014 yards <> $$
34028 Electric Road - Corvallis, OR
541-752-3332 - Reservations Advised
www.trystingtree.com

This challenging year-round course opened in 1988, and has been called one of the top ten public courses in the state by Golf Digest. Hazards include lots of water and plenty of mounds on this Scottish links-style course. With four sets of tees the distance ranges from 5516 to 7014 yards. During the spring and summer you can get on the course at 7am and they close at dusk; the rest of the year they do not open until 8am.

Green fees are $20 for 9 holes or $37 for 18 all week long. On Mondays and Tuesdays when you play before

1pm you'll pay $16 for 9 holes or $27 for 18. In-state college students pay $12 and $20 from mid-October until mid-March. Juniors 17 and younger pay $5 Monday thru Thursday and $10 the balance of the week. Motorized carts rent for $13 per 9 holes; the trail fee for bringing your own cart is $10.

Facilities include the Tree House Grille where you'll find hot food and cold Northwest beer and wine, plus a full-service pro shop and a 300-yard driving range with three target greens. Lessons, and help with tournament planning, are available.

Directions: Take Highway 34 west of I-5 about 9 miles to Trysting Tree.

Cottage Grove

Hidden Valley Golf Course
9 Holes <> Par 35 <> Length 2803 yards <> $
775 N River Road - Cottage Grove, OR
541-942-3046 - Reservations Advised
www.playhiddenvalleygolf.com

The Hidden Valley course is pretty flat, but not easy; you'll encounter two par 5's in your first four holes. The old oaks are huge and the course is edged by both a creek and river, giving you lots of natural hazards.

Designed by Ray Vincent, the fairway has two sets of tees so you can play 18 holes with variety; the slope is 120-125 and the ratings 66.5-67.6.

Open year round, dawn to dusk, the women's par is 35 for a total distance of 2375 yards. This course was first introduced in 1929, making it one of the oldest in Oregon. Facilities include a restaurant and lounge with banquet facilities, and a full-service pro shop.

Weekday green fees are $12 for 9 holes or $17 for 18; seniors and students play for $10 and $15. On weekends and holidays it's $14 and $20, with juniors, age 17 and under, playing for $8 and $12. Every day of the week the twilight special begins at 4pm and rates drop to $10 and $15 for everyone. Clubs rent for $3 per 9 holes, handcarts are $2 and $3, and motorized carts $15 for 9 holes or $20 for 18. The trail fee, when you bring your own cart, is $4 and $6.

Directions: Leave I-5 at exit #174 and follow the signs. From Highway 99 heading south you turn right at the first signal onto Woodson. The course is behind the Elks Lodge.

Middlefield Village Golf Course
18 Holes <> Par 67 <> Length 5002 yards <> $
91 Village Drive - Cottage Grove, OR
541-942-8730 - Reservations Needed
www.middlefieldgolf.com

When you play the softly rolling fairways at Middlefield, you'll encounter a sporty executive course lined with trees. Built in 1991, beginning players will like this course because it's not too long; better golfers will enjoy the interesting layout. Situated along the Row River, and open year round, it was designed by Bunny Mason.

Weekend green fees are $18 for 9 holes and $28 for 18; on weekdays you'll pay $16 and $25. Seniors and college students pay $14 and $20 during the week, juniors $8 and $12.

Twilight rates are available on non-holiday weekdays; those rates are $12 and $18 with seniors saving an additional $2 on 18 holes.

November thru February adults pay $10 for 9 holes or $15 for 18; juniors pay a flat $5. Clubs rent for $7, pull carts are $3, and clubs are $12 for 9 holes or $20 for 18.

Facilities include a full-service pro shop, driving range, and a deli where you can get cold beer. They also have an on-site golf school and offer both individual and group lessons.

At the driving range grass tees are available during golf seasons; in the winter you practice from covered Astroturf.

Directions: Leave I-5 on exit #174 and go east 2 blocks, turn left, and follow the signs.

Creswell

Emerald Valley Golf Club
18 Holes <> Par 72 <> Length 6388 yards <> $$
83301 Dale Kuni Road - Creswell, OR
541-895-2174 - Reservations Suggested
www.evgolfresort.com

Built in 1966, and designed by Bob Baldock, this course has bent grass fairways and greens. The Oregon Golf Association named this "Golf Course of the Year" in 2004. Three of the par 4's at Emerald Valley have a reputation for being among the most difficult holes in Oregon. The slope is 126 and the course rating 73.0.

Open year round, this course was built in 1964. The fairways are level to gently rolling with three sets of tees. The total yardage from the women's tees is 6371 for a par of 73.

Weekend rates are set for Friday thru Sunday as well as all major holidays. On weekends you'll pay $30 for 9 holes or $50 for 18; Monday thru Thursday you'll pay $25 and $45. Juniors, age 17 and under, pay $15 no matter how many holes they play. Students age 18 to 24, and seniors age 60 and older, receive a $5 discount off 18-hole rates. Carts rent for $15 per 9 holes.

Facilities include a pro shop and driving range.

Directions: Leave I-5 at the Creswell exit and go east on Cloverdale Road to Dale Kuni Road and the course.

Dallas

Sandstrip Golf Course
9 Holes <> Par 31 <> Length 2031 yards <> $$
11875 Orrs Corner Road - Dallas, OR
503-623-6832 - Reservations Advised

Sandstrip is fairly flat with some trees and water. Built in 1989, it was designed by John Zoller and Bruce Perisho. This is a challenging executive course with small greens. The slope is 91, the rating 58.2, and the course is open year round.

Green fees for 9 holes are $30 on weekends and $25 during the week all year round. For 18 holes you'll pay $40-45 midweek and $45-50 on weekends depending on the season. Twilight rates, October thru April, are $35 all week long. Juniors play for $15 year round; seniors save $5 on regular rates. Rental clubs are $14, handcarts $3, and motorized carts are $15 per 9 holes.

They have lots of activity days going on at Emerald Valley, some year round, some only during specific months; Tightwad Tuesday, Burger & Brew Wednesdays, Super Twilight, Nine & Wine Ladies League and Couples Golf all offer special rates.

Facilities include the Front Nine Restaurant and Back Nine Bar; Northwest food, beer, and wine are their specialty. Sandstrip also has chipping and putting greens, and a driving range with both mat and grass tees; you can get a bucket of balls for $5, $7 and $10, depending on how many you need. Ask at the pro shop for help with tournament planning or golf lessons.

Directions: Take Highway 22 to Highway 99S and follow this for 3 miles to the N. Kings Valley Hwy exit. After 1 mile angle left on Oak Villa Rd for 1.2 miles, turn left onto Ellendale Ave for .5 mile, take the first right onto SE Fir Villa Rd, go .6 mile and turn left onto Orrs Corner Road. The course is .2 mile.

Eagle Creek

Eagle Creek Golf Course
18 Holes <> Par 70 <> Length 6296 yards <> $
25805 SE Dowty Road - Eagle Creek, OR
503-630-4676 - Reservations Required

Eagle Creek opened in 1994 and has unspoiled forests, a winding stream and wildlife. The terrain is flat with lots of oak and fir trees. You'll encounter lots of water, sand traps, and might even spot some wildlife during your game.

You'll find scenic views of Mt. Hood too. The 5th hole is 633 yards, takes you over a pond for a par five, and has a well-earned reputation for being one of the state's most difficult holes. The course is open year round, from dawn to dusk.

During the week you can play 9 holes at Eagle Creek for $10-12; 18 will cost you $18-22, depending on the season. Clubs rent for $5 per 9 holes, handcarts $2, and motorized carts $12. Amenities include a putting green and snack bar.

Directions: Take Highway 224 to Eagle Creek and follow the signs. They will take you 1.7 miles along Folsom Road and 1.1 miles down Dowty Road to the course road.

Eagle Point

Eagle Point Golf Course
18 Holes <> Par 72 <> Length 7096 yards <> $$
100 Eagle Point Drive - Eagle Point, OR
541-826-8225
www.eaglepointgolf.com

This semi-private golf course has great drainage and is open to the public. Designed by Robert Trent Jones, Jr., and opened in 1996, this course has a spectacular layout and four sets of tees. Total distance ranges from 6101 to 7096 yards; the slope is 118 to 135 and the ratings 69.5 to 74.1. Eagle Point was ranked 11th in the state by the Oregon Golf Association.

Green fees during peak season are $42 during the week and $50 on weekends; off season you'll pay $32 all week long. Junior golfer, age 17 and under, can play any time of the year for $15. Twilight discounts start at noon off season; the cost is $25. Golf carts rent for $13 per rider; during twilight carts are $10 per rider.

Facilities include a 15,000 square foot state-of-the-art practice facility with grass mats. There is also a short game practice area, chipping areas and a practice bunker. The clubhouse includes a terrific place to eat, Arthur's Restaurant, and a full-service bar. The golf shop carries a full line of equipment and clothing; they can also help with tournament planning and lessons.

Directions: Located 10 miles east of Medford, in Eagle Point. Follow Highway 62 east; in Eagle Point take Shasta Avenue to Alta Vista Road. After .6 mile you will come to Eagle Point Drive.; follow this to the course.

Stone Ridge Golf Club
18 Holes <> Par 72 <> Length 6738 yards <> $$
500 E Antelope Road - Eagle Point, OR
541-830-4653 - Reservations Available

Opened in 1995, Stone Ridge is a year-round course with a slope of 132 from the back tees for a rating of 72.5. You'll find a lot of variety here with some par threes sporting as many as eight separate tee boxes. The terrain has some hills, tree-lined fairways and good views; fairways are planted with Bermuda grass and the greens bent grass. The 16th hole has a waterfall. Designed by Jim Cochran, from the ladies' tees the total distance is 4986 yards.

December thru February green fees for 18 holes are $39 on weekdays, $46 on weekends, and $30 at twilight. March thru November 18 holes will cost you $55 on weekdays, $63 on weekends, and $42 at twilight. Motorized carts rent for $10 per 9 holes, clubs rent for $25, and pull carts are available.

Facilities include a snack bar where you'll find cold beer, a covered outdoor banquet area, chipping and putting greens, a 15,000-square-foot state of the art practice facility with grass and mat tees, and full-service pro shop. Help with tournament planning, and lessons, is available.

Directions: Leave I-5 at exit #30 and go east on Hwy 62 for 6 miles to Hwy 140; turn right and drive 3 miles to East Antelope Road and the course.

Estacada

Springwater Golf Course
9 Holes <> Par 36 <> Length 3003 yards <> $
25230 S Wallens Road - Estacada, OR
503-630-4586 - Reservations Needed

The Springwater course is situated in a picturesque spot with a great view of both Mt. Hood and Mount St. Helens. Open year round, it is flat with some hills, has good drainage, and is a good place for winter golf. Water comes into play on two holes, and the 3rd hole includes a dogleg and a hill for a 384 yard par 4.

The slope is 120 and the ratings 67.9 for men, and 72.8 for women. From the ladies tees the total distance is 2479 yards. Men and women each have two sets of tees, adding variety to an 18-hole game.

During the week green fees are $12 for 9 holes or $22 for 18. On weekends and holidays it'll cost you $14 or $26. On weekdays golfers over age 60, and those in high school or younger, can play for discounted rates. Clubs, hand carts and motorized carts are available.

Facilities include a snack bar that offers beer and wine, plus a pro shop and practice green. Lessons are available.

Directions: Located 4 miles south of Estacada; leave Hwy. 211 on Wallens Road and follow it to the course.

Eugene

Fiddler's Green Golf Course
18 Holes <> Par 54 <> Length 2378 yards <> $
91292 Highway 99N - Eugene, OR

541-689-8464
www.fiddlersgreen.com/golfcourse

Fiddler's Green is one of Oregon's finest par three courses and offers level, easy walking. Designed by John Zoller Sr., it opened in 1963. Children are not permitted on the course or driving range unless they are golfing.

A year-round course, summer green fees are $9 for 9 holes or $15 for 18. Seniors, age 62 and over, pay $7 and $12. Juniors, age 15 and under, also play for $7 and $12. Clubs rent for $3.50 and handcarts are $3. On the driving range you'll pay $1.50 for 30 balls.

Facilities include a lighted driving range with mat tees that offers both covered and open turf. You'll also find an indoor video lesson studio with four cameras to help you monitor your performance, personalized instruction, a full-service pro shop, and a snack bar where beer and wine is available.

Directions: Fiddler's Green is located on Highway 99N, 2 miles north of the airport. From I-5 take the Beltline Road exit, #195, and go north 5 miles. Follow Hwy. 99 toward the airport and the golf course.

Laurelwood Golf Course
9 Holes <> Par 35 <> Length 3061 yards <> $
2700 Columbia - Eugene, OR
541-687-5321 - Reservations Advised
www.golflaurelwood.com

The Laurelwood course opened in 1929 as Eugene's first country club, and sits in the heart of the city. This course's 1st hole is considered to be one of the toughest holes in Oregon; it's a 540 yard par 5. This course has rolling hills, sloped greens, mature trees, and is rated 67.9 for men, 69.1 for women. Open year round, the total yardage from the women's tees is 2460.

Weekday green fees are $18 for 9 holes and $30 for 18 holes May 15th thru September. Juniors, age 17 and younger, play for $10, and seniors, age 62 and older, play 9 holes for $15 or 18 for $25 Monday thru Thursday.

October thru November, and March thru mid May, rates are $15 for 9 holes or $25 for 18, juniors pay $10, and seniors and students pay $12 and $20. December thru February everyone pays $10 for 9 holes or $15 for 18. Motorized carts rent for $15 and $25.

Facilities include a full-service pro shop where you can get a cold beer, plus a driving range with mat tees. At the range you get a bucket of balls for $3.50, $7 and $10.50, depending on the size of the bucket. They can provide help with tournament planning, as well as golf lessons, club repair, and custom clubs.

Directions: Leave I-5 northbound at the 30th Ave exit and turn right onto Hilyard. Go right again on 24th and follow the signs. From I-5 southbound take the Eugene exit, follow the signs to Franklin Blvd, turn right onto Agate, left on onto 24th, and follow the signs.

Oakway Golf Course

18 Holes <> Par 61 <> Length 3241 yards <> $
2000 Cal Young Road - Eugene, OR
541-484-1927
www.oakwaygolf.com

Designed by John Zoller, Oakway was built in 1983 and is open year round, weather permitting. Its terrain is slightly rolling, and the greens well kept, with some water, elevated tees, and lots of sand traps. The slope is 91 and the course rating 57.3. The total distance from the ladies' tees is 3117 yards.

Green fees at this executive 18-hole course are $14 for 9 holes and $22 for 18 midweek; weekend rates are $16 and $24. Juniors, age 17 and under, play for $8 and $12. Seven days a week seniors can play 9 holes for $12 or 18 for $18. Clubs rent for $7, handcarts $3, and motorized carts are $15.

You will find a restaurant where beer and wine is served, plus a full-service pro shop, two mat practice cages, a large putting green and practice area. They can also help with tournament planning and arrange for lessons.

Directions: Leave I-5 at I-105, head west to the Coburg Road exit, at the intersection turn right onto Oakway Road, follow this road to its end, and turn left to the golf course.

Riveridge Golf Course

36 Holes <> Par 71 <> Length 6256 yards <> $$
3800 N Delta Hwy. - Eugene, OR
541-345-9160 - Reservations Suggested

Riveridge is set along the Willamette River, and although fairly flat, does have some hills. This course will challenge golfers of all levels. It's an Audubon certified golf course and boasts over 120 species of trees. Course hours are 7am to 8pm year round.

Designed by Ric Jeffries, the 18-hole course was opened in 1988. With four sets of tees, the slope is 112 to 116, and the ratings range from 67.7 to 68.8. Two 9-hole courses are also found at this location. **Sutton Ridge** is a quick 9-hole executive course; **Short Ridge** is a par 3 9-hole course.

Green fees on the 18-hole Riveridge Course are $18 and $30 Monday thru Friday and $19 and $32 on weekends and holidays. Seniors, age 60 and over, play for $13 and $22 on weekdays, $19 and $32 on weekends and holidays. After 2pm seniors qualify to play for weekday rates. Juniors, age 17 and under, can play 9 holes on weekends and holidays for $17; the rest of the week they pay $7.50. Golf carts rent for $15 and $26; pull carts are $5.

On SuttonRidge rates are the same 7 days a week, $14. Juniors play for $7.50 and seniors $11. The Short Ridge course is $6.50. Cart fees are the same on all three courses.

Facilities include a driving range, plus a snack bar where beer and wine is available, and a full-service pro shop. Lessons are offered and you can get help with tournament planning. At the driving range you'll find 27 covered stalls and 10 uncovered. You can get a bucket of balls for $4.50, $7.25 and $10.

Directions: Take Delta Highway 1 mile north of Beltline.

Forest Grove

Sunset Grove Golf Club
9 Holes <> Par 36 <> Length 3001 yards <> $
41569 NW Osterman - Forest Grove, OR
503-357-6044 - Reservations Advised

The Sunset Grove course has a rolling terrain, fairly small greens, wide fairways, two water holes, and a view of Mt. Hood off the 7th tee. It is open year round, and a good course for beginning golfers. The women's par is 37 for a total distance of 2715 yards. The slope from the championship tees is 107 for a rating of 34.

Green fees are $14 for 9 holes during the week and $24 on weekends during peak season. Off season you'll pay $11 and $20. Monday thru Friday juniors and seniors can play for reduced rates. Motorized carts rent for $12, clubs are $3.50, and handcarts are $2.

Facilities include a chipping and putting green, snacks, and a bar. They have a limited pro shop where you can get help with lessons.

Directions: Located 2 miles north of town on Highway 47.

Gold Hill

Laurel Hill Golf Course
9 Holes <> Par 31 <> Length 1915 yards <> $
9450 Old Stage Road - Gold Hill, OR
541-855-7965
www.laurelhillgolf.com

Laurel Hill was designed by Harvey Granger and opened in 1977. It operates year round and provides a challenging game that is played across a relative flat terrain with lots of trees. Four par 4's and a couple of tree-lined doglegs make this a difficult course. The 9th hole has a pond as well as a dogleg.

The slope is 102 and ratings 61.5 for men, 62.3 for women. Two sets of tees are available. Located in a valley, and surrounded by mountains, it's an easy-to-walk scenic course. The shortest hole is 110 yards; the longest hole is 310 yards.

Weekday green fees are $10 for 9 holes or $15 for 18; on weekends and holidays you'll pay $10.50 and $17. Juniors play for $7 and $12 on weekdays, $7.50 and $14 on weekends. Seniors pay $9 and $14 weekdays and $9.50 and $16.50 on weekends and holidays. Motorized carts rent for $7 and $12 if there is only one rider, $10 and $18 for two. They have a limited pro shop with a snack bar that offers cold beer.

Directions: Take exit #40 off I-5; the course is just a short distance west of the freeway.

Grants Pass

Applegate River Golf Club
9 Holes <> Par 36 <> Length 2643 yards <> $
7350 New Hope Road - Grants Pass, OR
541-955-0480 - Reservations Required
www.applegaterivergolfclub.com

This course was designed by John T. Briggs and opened late in 1994. The slope is 104 with a rating of 65.8 for men, 114 and 69.8 for women. You'll find water on 8 holes, a flat terrain, plenty of natural trees, and a dogleg on the 6th hole with a par four. The fairways are wide open and the setting gorgeous. Open year round, dawn to dusk, an early golfer might spot deer or osprey on this course. The total distance from other tees are 2205 and 2492 yards.

Green fees are $14 for 9 holes or $19 for 18; seniors play for $12 and $17. Junior rates are $5 per 9 holes. Clubs rent for $5-10, pull carts are $2, and motorized carts are $8 and $11.

Facilities include a snack bar where you can get cold beer and wine, plus a lounge, driving range, and pro shop. Lessons, and help with tournament planning, are available. At the driving range you'll pay $2.50, $4 and $6 for a bucket of balls, depending on how many you want.

Direction: Leave I-5 on Highway 238 and head south 7 miles to Murphy, then follow New Hope Road 1.2 miles to the course.

Dutcher Creek Golf Course
18 Holes <> Par 70 <> Length 5588 yards <> $$
4611 Upper River Road - Grants Pass, OR
541-474-2188 - Reservations Available
www.dutchercreekgolf.com

Dutcher Creek is a links-style course with bent grass greens. Open dawn to dusk, year round, it has a nice mountain view and a creek running through the course. Water comes into play on 7 holes. The slope is 118 with a rating of 66.7. Four sets of tees are available. The total yardage from the ladies tees is 4605.

Green fees are $18 for 9 holes or $25 for 18 seven days a week. Seniors, age 55 and older, play for $15 and $19. Twilight rates start at 4pm. Clubs rent for $12, handcarts are $2, and motorized carts $8-14 per rider.

Facilities include a chipping and putting green, driving cages, and a pro shop where you can get snacks, arrange lessons, and get help with tournament planning. On the practice range you'll pay $2-5 for a bucket of balls.

Directions: Leave downtown on G Street, which soon becomes Upper River Road; follow this road for 4 miles.

Grants Pass Golf Club
18 Holes <> Par 72 <> Length 6381 yards <> $$
230 Espey Road - Grants Pass, OR
541-476-0849 - Reservations Required
www.grantspassgolfclub.com

This course has a flat front nine with lots of water, and a hilly forested back nine. A semi-private course, they are closed to the public until noon Friday thru Tuesday, prior to 1pm on Wednesdays, and before 1:30pm on Thursdays. The front nine was built in 1946; the back nine in 1973. The 12th hole is the signature hole. The total distance from the shortest tees is 5121 yards.

Green fees are $30 for 9 holes or $50 for 18. Clubs can be rented for $8; motorized carts are $16 for 9 holes or

$25 for 18. Facilities include a chipping and putting green, restaurant with a liquor license, a driving range, and full-service pro shop. Lessons can be arranged, and they offer help with tournament planning. The driving range has both grass and mat tees.

Directions: Take Highway 238 south of Grants Pass for 3 miles to Espey Road.

Red Mountain Golf Course
9 Holes <> Par 28 <> Length 1118 yards <> $
324 N Schoolhouse Creek Road - Grants Pass, OR
541-479-2297 - Reservations Available

The Red Mountain course is located just north of Grants Pass, in the Hugo Hills. This challenging executive nine is open year round, sunrise to sunset. Designed by Robert and Dave Snook, the course opened in 1988. You'll find a scenic setting with rolling hills, lots of trees, and water. Walk-ons are welcome.

Green fees are $11 for 9 holes March thru October; the rest of the year it will cost you $10. Seniors play for $10 during peak season and $9 the rest of the year.

They have a nice clubhouse where you will find cold beer and wine, plus limited banquet facilities, a snack bar, and a small pro shop. Driving nets are provided, as is help with tournament planning.

Directions: Leave I-5 at the Merlin exit #61, head under the freeway, turn right onto Monument Drive, and after

3.6 miles turn right onto Potts Way. Follow this for an additional mile to the course.

Independence

Oak Knoll Golf Course
18 Holes <> Par 72 <> Length 6208 yards <> $
6335 Highway 22 - Independence, OR
503-363-6652 - Reservations Advised
www.oakknollgolfcourse.com

There has been a golf course at this location since 1926. Oak Knoll offers a flat to rolling terrain, has three ponds, and a nice view of the Coast Mountains. The slope is 111 and the ratings 67.1 for men, and 69.2 for women. Open 7am to dusk year round, the total distance from the women's tees is 5239 yards.

Green fees are $18 for 9 holes or $30 for 18 on weekends and holidays. Tuesday thru Friday you'll pay $16 or $28; on Mondays rates drop to $12 and $20. Seniors play for $15 and $26 Tuesday thru Friday, and juniors $8 and $14. College students play for $12 and $22. Motorized carts rent for $7 and $13 per rider.

You'll find a restaurant and lounge with a liquor license, help with tournament planning, and a driving range at Oak Knoll. They offer group and private lessons. At the driving range they have both covered mats and grass tees. You get a small bucket of balls for $2, medium for $3, or a large one for $4. The range is open from 7am to dusk.

Directions: To find the course, leave I-5 at the Highway 22-Ocean Beaches exit. This will take you through Salem. Head west 7 miles to the course.

King City

King City Golf Club
9 Holes <> Par 34 <> Length 2415 yards <> $
15355 SW Royalty Pkwy. - King City, OR
503-639-7986 - Reservations Recommended
www.kingcitygolf.com

The King City course is flat, narrow, and surrounded by trees and houses. A semi-private course, it is open year round, but closed to the public on Wednesday and Thursday mornings before 11am. Many golfers consider King City's 7th hole one of the finest in the state. It is 415 yards for a par four and includes 5 traps; the lake sits 40 yards in front of the green. Built in 1966, the women's par is 35 for a total distance of 2347 yards.

Green fees for non residents are $15 all week long; the second nine will cost you $13. Clubs rent for $5, pull carts are $2, and power carts $10 for one person or $12 for two. You'll find a full-service pro shop, snacks, and a driving net. Ask at the pro shop for help with tournament planning or to arrange for lessons.

Directions: To get to the King City Golf Course, take the Tigard exit off I-5 and drive thru Tigard to King City. You'll find the course just past the city limits.

Leaburg

McKenzie River Golf Course
9 Holes <> Par 36 <> Length 2803 yards <> $
41723 Madrone - Leaburg, OR
541-896-3454 - Reservations Advised
www.mckenzierivergolf.com

This year-round course was built in 1961 and is situated along the McKenzie River. The terrain is flat with only one hill, making it easy to walk. Two sets of tees provide variety when playing 18 holes. The slope is 107 and the course rating 33.0. They are open from dawn to dusk.

A 9-hole game will cost you $13 on weekdays or $16 on weekends; 18 holes are $24 and $28. Power carts are $13 for 9 holes or $25 for 18, and pull carts rent for $2. Facilities include a pro shop, snack bar, practice putting green, and a covered driving range. Golf lessons and help with tournament planning are available.

Directions: Located 10 miles northeast of Springfield via Highway 126, .5 mile beyond milepost #117.

Lebanon

Mallard Creek Golf Course
18 Holes <> Par 00 <> Length 7000 yards <> $$
31966 Bellinger Scale Road - Lebanon, OR
541-259-4653
www.mallardcreekgc.com

This 18-hole course makes its way alongside several lakes, around stands of old trees, travels around and across Hamilton Creek, and makes its way through rolling hills. Opened in 2000, it has bent grass greens and fairways, and utilizes the natural terrain to keep the game interesting.

During peak season green fees are $25 for 9 holes or $47 for 18 Friday thru Sunday, and on all holidays. Monday thru Thursday you'll pay $22 or $40. Motorized carts rent for $13 and $26.

Facilities include a full-service pro shop and a covered driving range offering both grass and artificial tees. You'll find a practice sand bunker, as well as putting and chipping greens. The Grill at Mallard Creek offers food and alcohol; they also have a full line of Pacific Northwest microbrews. This is also a RV Resort with 43 sites and full hookups.

Directions: Leave I-5 on exit #228, the Corvallis/Lebanon exit. Follow Hwy 34 east to Lebanon and turn right onto Hwy 20. After .5 mile turn onto Grant St, cross over the Santiam River, and take a hard right onto Berlin Road. Follow this for 6.1 miles; the golf course is on the left.

Pineway Golf Course
9 Holes <> Par 36 <> Length 2967 yards <> $
30949 Pineway Road - Lebanon, OR
541-258-8815 - Reservations Advised

Pineway is slightly hilly with elevated greens and was built in 1958. Nestled in the side of a hill, it offers a particularly beautiful setting with a wonderful view of the Cascade Mountains. Open year round, large trees line the fairways and ponds come into play on three holes. The course rating is 34 with a slope of 108.

Green fees remain the same seven days a week, $15 for 9 holes or $25 for 18. Monday thru Friday seniors play for $13 and $20; juniors pay $10 and $20. You can rent clubs for $7; pull carts are $3, and motorized carts $15 for 9 holes or $25 for 18.

Facilities include putting and chipping greens, a practice bunker, driving range, and a pro shop where you can get help with tournament planning and lessons. You'll find a restaurant and lounge with a liquor license and a great view of the golf course. You can get a bucket of balls at the driving range for $3 to $5.

Directions: Located 3.5 miles east of town on Highway 20.

Lyons

Elkhorn Valley Golf Club
18 Holes <> Par 71 <> Length 6242 yards <> $$
North Fork Road - Lyons, OR
503-897-3368 - Reservations Recommended
www.elkhorngolf.com

It took Don Cutler 11 years to build this course, but when it opened in 1976 most area golfers agreed it was worth the wait. Situated in a beautiful mountain valley, it offers a view of eight mountain peaks. The slope is 136 and the ratings 71.4 for men, 63.6 for women.

Elkhorn has four tees for every hole and is one of the best 9-hole courses in the United States. The 6th hole requires you to get your ball across a canyon for a par three; a second canyon, plus plenty of water, makes this course very challenging. The terrain is flat and easy to walk, and the course is open March thru October. The total yardage from the ladies tees is 2445.

Green fees during peak season for 9 holes of play are $16-21 on weekdays, $25-30 with a cart. On weekends 9 holes are $21-26, $30-$35 with a cart. For 18 holes you'll pay $26-35 during the week and $35-40 on weekends; add a cart and those rates go up to $35-49 during the week and $49-54 on weekends. Twilight rates start at 3pm; rates are $20 without a cart, $30 with a cart. You'll find cold snacks, sandwiches, beer and wine in the pro shop.

Directions: To find Elkhorn Valley, from Lyons, take North Fork Road east 11 miles.

Medford

Bear Creek Golf Course
9 Holes <> Par 29 <> Length 1601 yards <> $
2355 S Pacific Hwy. - Medford, OR
541-773-1822 - Reservations Available
www.golfbearcreek.com

Bear Creek is a sporty little course. The slope is 95 and the course rating 57.0. Open year round, it has both a lake and a creek which will help to keep your game sharp. A fast course, it sits in a valley and has a beautiful view of snow-capped mountains. Par from the ladies' tees is 30.

Green fees are $14 for 9 holes or $20 for 18 on weekends and holidays, $12 and $18 the balance of the week. Juniors pay $7 for 9 holes or $13 for 18 seven days a week. They also offer all day play rates and special days when seniors, active military members and juniors play for discounted rates; check the website for current specials.

Facilities include a deli where you'll find cold beer and wine, plus a full-service pro shop, covered driving range, putting greens, and an 18-hole miniature golf course. Lessons are available.

Directions: Leave I-5 southbound on the Barnett exit and take Pacific Highway south 1 mile.

Cedar Links Golf Club
9 Holes <> Par 36 <> Length 3327 yards <> $
3155 Cedar Links Drive - Medford, OR
541-773-4373 - Reservations Available

You'll find a rolling terrain at Cedar Links, plus a great view of the Rogue Valley and surrounding mountains. Its slope is 123 and the course rating 35.5. Open every day but Christmas, the women's tees have a distance of 2749 yards. This was once an 18-hole course, you are playing the old back nine.

Green fees are $14 for 9 holes or $24 for 18 during the week; $16 and $26 on weekends and holidays. Clubs are available for $7, handcarts $3, and motorized carts $12 and $24. On the driving range you can get 40 balls for $3.

Facilities include a putting green, chipping area, a restaurant with a liquor license, plus banquet rooms, a full-service pro shop, and a driving range. The driving range has mat tees. Lessons, and help with tournament planning, are available.

Directions: Follow Cedar Links Drive.

Centennial Golf Club

18 Holes <> Par 72 <> Length 7309 yards <> $$$$
1900 N Phoenix Road - Medford, OR
541-773-4653 - Reservations Required
www.centennialgolfclub.com

Centennial was designed by John Fought and opened in 2006. Situated at the site of a historic pear orchard, the course is relatively flat with four ponds. You'll find four par 5's, ten 4's, and four 3's, enough to challenge any golfer.

Green fees Friday thru Sunday, and holidays, are $73 for 18 holes; the rest of the week it's $63. Jackson, Josephine, Douglas and Klamath County residents can play for $53; $46 Monday thru Thursday. Golf carts are $10 for 9 holes or $14 for 18 holes, per rider.

Facilities include a restaurant, clubhouse, pro shop, driving range, and banquet facilities. Private and group lessons are available.

Directions: Leave I-5 northbound on exit #27 for Barnett Road and follow Barnett for 2 miles to North Phoenix Road; turn right and go 1 mile to the course.

Quail Point Golf Course

9 Holes <> Par 35 <> Length 1872 yards <> $
1200 Mira Mar Avenue - Medford, OR
541-857-7000 - Reservations Advised
www.quailpointgolf.com

This year-round course was designed by Bob Foster, and opened in 1993. Winter hours are 8am to dusk; the rest of the year they open at 7am. A hilly course, you'll find lots of trees, plenty of water, and four sets of tees. The 4th hole has a stream and sand traps with a pond on one side, the 8th hole has water on three sides of the green, and the 9th is surrounded by a lake. It's a challenging little course.

Green fees are $18 for 9 holes or $28 for 18 all week long; a cart will add $10 or $14 per person. Twilight rates begin at 3pm when 9-hole rates drop to $14 and 18-holes cost $20. Clubs rent for $10 and $15, and pull carts are $2 and $3. Monday thru Thursday seniors play for $12 and $18; cart fees add $8-12 per person.

Facilities include a chipping area, pro shop, and an 18-hole putting course that's perfect for family fun. Adults pay $5 for 9 holes or $8 for 18; kids 17 and under are just $3 and $5, on the putting course.

Directions: Leave I-5 on Barnett and head east, take a right on Black Oak, right on Mira Mar, and turn right again on Shannon.

Stewart Meadows Golf Course
9 Holes <> Par 35 <> Length 2910 yards <> $$
1301 S Holly Street - Medford, OR
541-770-6554 - Reservations Available
www.stewardmeadows.com

Steward Meadows is flat and easy to walk with lots of mounds, four large ponds, dozens of sand traps, and hundreds of trees. A year-round course, it was designed by Chuck Magnum and opened in 1993. Winter hours are 7:30am to dusk; they open at 6:30am the balance of the year. From the ladies tees the total yardage is 2800.

Green fees are the same all week long, $16 for 9 holes or $25 for 18. Seniors can play for $13 and $20 Monday thru Thursday. Juniors play for $7 and $13 all week long. Motorized carts rent for $14 and $22.

Facilities include a cafe and lounge where you can get cold beer and wine, plus a full-service pro shop. Lessons are available, and they also have a lighted driving range.

Directions: To find Stewart Meadows Golf Course leave I-5 on Barnett and turn right. After about .5 mile turn left on Holly and go 2 blocks to the course.

McMinnville

Bayou Golf Course

18 Holes <> Par 36 <> Length 3154 yards <> $
9301 SW Bayou Drive - McMinnville, OR
503-472-4651 - Reservations Required
www.bayougolfcourse.com

Bayou has both a short par three and a more challenging nine-hole course. That second course has a slope of 118 and ratings of 70.2 for men, 68.2 for women. Fairly flat, but challenging, it is situated on a gently rolling river delta with the South Yamhill River along its southern edge. On the 3rd hole you have the option to shoot across a pond for an additional challenge. The Bayou course is closed only on Christmas and Thanksgiving.

Par 3 green fees are $10 for 9 holes all week long; seniors play for $8. On the longer course they are $20 and $30 on weekends and holidays, $18 and $28 the rest of the week. Clubs can be rented for $10, handcarts $2, and motorized carts $13 and $23.

Facilities include putting and chipping practice areas, and a southern-style mansion that houses a snack bar, where you'll find beer and wine, and a banquet room. They also have a driving range and full service pro shop where you can arrange for lessons and get help with tournament planning. The driving range is open March thru October, offers grass tees, and balls are $3 for 35.

Directions: Bayou is located 1 mile south of McMinnville, along Highway 99W.

Mt. Angel

Evergreen Golf Club
9 Holes <> Par 36 <> Length 3044 yards <> $
11694 W Church Road NE - Mt. Angel, OR
503-845-9911 - Reservations Advised
www.evergreenoregon.com

The terrain at Evergreen is rolling, but not hilly, making it easy to walk. It is well maintained, and the course is open year round. Built in 1962, the slope is 110 and the rating 68.6. The women's par is 37 for a total distance of 2737 yards.

You'll find lots of trees, a small pond, and a beautiful view of Mt. Hood. The 4th and 7th holes will challenge your short game; the distance is 118 and 144 yards. Men have the course all to themselves on Thursday mornings; the ladies get it on Tuesday mornings.

Green fees are $13 for 9 holes and $23 for 18 during the week; on the weekends it'll cost you $15 and $26. During the winter a 9-hole game will cost you $12. Juniors and seniors can play during the week for $11 and $20. Power carts rent for $12 and $22; seniors who golf on weekdays pay only $10 and $18. Clubs can be rented for $10 and handcarts are $3.

Facilities include a restaurant and lounge with a liquor license, and banquet rooms. You can arrange for lessons at the full-service pro shop, and get help with tournament planning. Evergreen also has a nice "start your own golf league" program, making it easy for groups to get together.

Directions: Church Road is near the junction of Main Street and Wilcox; take this road 1.5 miles east of town.

Mulino

Ranch Hills Golf Course
9 Holes <> Par 36 <> Length 2895 yards <> $
26710 S Ranch Hills Road - Mulino, OR
503-632-6848 - Reservations Advised

Ranch Hills is pretty with a creek winding its way through the middle of the course, and its own covered bridge. The terrain is flat and challenging, with winter rye fairways; the course is open year round. Three sets of tees are available. From the blue tees the slope is 100 with a rating of 64.0. From the women's tees the total distance is 2636 yards for a par of 37.

The Northwest Golfer: Oregon Edition

During the week you'll pay $14.50 for 9 holes; on weekends it'll cost you $1 more. For 18 holes you'll pay $27 and $29. Juniors and seniors play for $10.50 and $19. Clubs are available for $15, handcarts $2, and motorized carts $12 per 9 holes.

Facilities include a full-service pro shop, putting green, driving range, and a snack bar where you can purchase cold beer and wine. Lessons, and help with tournament planning, are available.

Directions: Take Molalla Avenue south of Oregon City; after 9 miles turn left on Passmore and follow the signs.

Oakridge

Circle Bar Golf Course
9 Holes <> Par 36 <> Length 3281 yards <> $
48447 Westoak Road - Oakridge, OR
541-782-3541 - Reservations Suggested
www.circlebargolf.org

This year-round course has a flat terrain with a few good hills and plenty of water. It sits in a valley, surrounded by hills, at an elevation of 1200'. Open year round, this is one of Lane County's most difficult 9-hole courses. Circle Bar opened in the early 1950's, has a slope of 119, and ratings of 70.8 for men, and 73.0 for women.

At 567 yards, the 4th hole is a real challenge, with a couple of ponds, trees, and an uphill finish. You'll find three tees per hole; the ladies tees have a par of 37 for a total distance of 2985 yards. Summer hours are 8am to 6pm, the balance of the year they're open 9am to 5pm.

Weekday green fees are $10 for 9 holes or $15 for 18. On weekends you'll pay $15 and $20. Facilities include a club house, and a limited pro shop with a snack bar offering cold beer and wine. The clubhouse has a spacious banquet room. Lessons, and help with tournament planning, are available.

Directions: Located in Oakridge, right on Highway 58; watch for the signs.

Oregon City

Oregon City Golf Club
18 Holes <> Par 71 <> Length 5864 yards <> $
20124 S Beavercreek Road - Oregon City, OR
503-518-2846 - Reservations Advised
www.ocgolfclub.com

This is one of Oregon's oldest golf courses; the original nine holes were built in 1922. In 1960 a second nine was added. Carved from the orchards and farmland of the Lone Oak Farm, this Oregon City course is a good winter courses. Because the terrain is mostly flat, and drains well, it is often playable when others are soggy. The slope is 107 and the ratings 67.3 for men, 70.8 for women. This course is open from dawn to dusk, 365 days out of the year. The women's par is 75.

Weekday green fees are $15 for 9 holes or $28 for 18; on weekends and holidays it's $20 and $36. Seniors, age 62 and older, can play during the week for $12 and $22; juniors play for $11 and $20. Clubs rent for $10, handcarts $3, and motorized carts $15 and $25; Monday thru Friday seniors pay $9 and $17 for a cart.

You can arrange for private or group lessons, and get help with tournaments at the pro shop. You will also find a snack bar offering cold sandwiches and beer.

Directions: Located 1 mile south of Clackamas Community College, on Beavercreek Road. From I-205 take the Molalla/Parkplace exit #10 and follow this for 3 miles to Beavercreek Road; turn left at this light and go an additional 1.5 miles to the golf course.

Stone Creek Golf Club
18 Holes <> Par 72 <> Length 6873 yards <> $$
14603 S Stoneridge Drive - Oregon City, OR
503-518-4653 - Reservations Available
www.stonecreekgolfclub.net

This course opened to the public in 2002, and was designed by Peter Jacobsen and Jim Hardy. Old-growth trees, wetlands, and lakes provide natural hazards; 43

bunkers add trouble. The front nine is links-style; the back nine is typical Pacific Northwest. The course rating is 73.2 with a slope of 132; from the ladies' tees the total distance is 5181 yards.

This course has three big ponds and a couple of creeks, as well as plenty of mature trees. The 11th hole is considered the most challenging tee shot, with a large bunker, and then Beaver Creek, to your right; the 13th hole has a difficult blind shot up a hill, the creek, and lots of large trees.

Green fees Friday thru Sunday, and holidays are $25 for 9 holes or $42 for 18; a cart adds $10-15 to the total. The rest of the week you'll pay $22 and $36; $31.25 and $51 if you add a cart. Early bird and twilight specials allow everyone to play for discounted rates. Clubs rent for $20-30, pull carts are $3 and $4, and motorized carts $10-15 per rider.

Monday thru Thursday seniors play for $15 and $25 when walking; it's $25 and $40 with a cart. The rest of the week seniors can play after 1pm for those same rates. Junior rates are $10 and $20 Monday thru Thursday; and after 1pm on weekends.

Facilities include a 6000-square-foot practice area; a bucket of balls will cost you $4-10 depending on how many you want. Putting and chipping greens, plus bunker practice areas and a large grass tee, along with qualified instructors, are all there to help you improve your game. The Stone Creek Deli offers sandwiches, cold drinks, and beer and wine.

THE NORTHWEST GOLFER: OREGON EDITION

Directions: From I-205, take exit #10 for Molalla and head south 6 miles. Turn right on Leland Road for .5 mile to Stoneridge Drive. The course is at the end of Stoneridge Drive.

Portland Area

(Beaverton)

Red Tail Golf Course

18 Holes <> Par 71 <> Length 6426 yards <> $$
8200 SW Scholls Ferry Road - Beaverton, OR
503-646-5166 - Reservations Advised
www.golfredtail.com

This is the old Progress Downs course. Built by the City of Portland Parks Department in 1969, it was upgraded in 2000 and re-opened to high praise. Six ponds, lots of trees, rolling hills and 45 bunkers, plus four sets of tees make this a challenging course. From the ladies tees the par is 73 for a total distance of 5626 yards.

Green fees for 9 holes Monday thru Thursday are $22; 18 holes will cost you $33. The rest of the week, and on all holidays, you'll pay $23 for 9 holes or $42 for 18. Juniors play for reduced rates; $11 and $21 during the week, $14 and $26 Friday thru Sunday. Seniors can play Monday thru Thursday for $17 and $30; $19 and $36 the rest of the week. Twilight rates start 3.5 hours prior to sundown for everybody; for $25-26 you can play all you want until the sun sets. Clubs rent for $20 and $30, carts are $3-5, and power carts $13-26.

Red Tail has a full-service pro shop with a large selection of products. Other amenities include a restaurant that serves classic grill food and cold beer, banquet facilities, a driving range, and a golf academy with a swing analyzer, video and still action equipment, and other helpful devices. They can assist you with tournament planning and arrange for everything from individual to group lessons.

At the driving range you'll pay $4.50 to $9 for balls, and they'll loan you clubs for free, while you're on the range.

Directions: From I-5, take Highway 217N at exit 292A towards Tigard and Beaverton. Take exit #4 to Scholls Ferry Road; the course is to the right on SW Scholls Ferry Road.

(Clackamas)

Sah-Hah-Lee Golf Course
18 Holes <> Par 54 <> Length 2477 yards <> $
17104 SE 130th Avenue - Clackamas, OR
503-655-9249 - Reservations Advised
www.sah-hah-lee.com

Built in 1990, this challenging course has winter rye fairways and bent grass greens. This is a good place for everyone from novice to advanced players. Located along the beautiful Clackamas River, this is a pretty course where deer, geese, and other wildlife abound. The clubhouse is an old farmhouse, and it overlooks the entire course.

Sah-hah-lee has been ranked among America's Top 100 Short Courses. Open from dawn to dark, year round, they close only on Christmas Day. The women's par is 73 for a total distance of 5626 yards.

During the week you'll pay $11 to play 9 holes or $18 for 18; on weekends they charge $12 and $20. Monday thru Friday they offer special rates to juniors and seniors; anyone younger than 16, or older than 59, can play 9 holes for $8 or 18 for $14.

Facilities include a snack bar offering beer and wine, plus a full-service pro shop, and covered driving range. The lighted range provides buckets of balls for $3.50 to $8, depending on how many balls you want.

They also have an 18-hole putting course; adults pay $5 and children younger than age 16 pay $4. The practice area is open until 10pm June thru August, 9pm March thru May, 8pm September thru October, and 7pm November thru February. Tournament planning and lessons can be arranged at the pro shop.

Directions: Take I-205 to the Highway 212 exit and drive east 2 miles before taking a right onto 130th Avenue. Follow this to the course.

(Cornelius)

Forest Hills Golf Course
18 Holes <> Par 72 <> Length 6173 yards <> $
36260 SW Tongue Lane - Cornelius
503-357-3347
www.golfforesthills.com

This year-round course offers great views of Mount St. Helens, Hood and Adams, tree-lined fairways, and a natural rolling terrain. Forest Hills was built in 1927; the course designer was William Bell. The slope is 114-117 and the ratings 66.7-69.2 for men, 122-126 and 70-73.6 for women. Par from the women's tees is 74 for a distance of 5673 yards.

Weekday green fees during peak season are $32 before 9am ($40 with a cart), and $36 after 9am ($50 with a cart). Weekends and holiday rates are $40 before 2pm or $32 after 2pm; add a cart and you'll pay $54 and $46.

During March and October everyone pays $15 for 9 holes or $32 for 18; a cart can be added for $14. November thru February it will cost you $15 and $30 to play, plus $14 for a cart.

Facilities include practice putting greens, a restaurant with a liquor license and banquet facilities, a driving range, and a full-service pro shop. They can help you with tournament planning and arrange for lessons; junior lessons are half the normal rate. At the driving range you'll find both mat and grass tees and you can get a bucket of balls for $2-7.

Directions: From Portland take Highway 26 west to exit #57, turn left on Glencoe Road, and follow this thru Hillsboro. The course is located 2.5 miles south of Hillsboro; turn right on Tongue Lane and follow 3 miles to the course.

Ghost Creek @ Pumpkin Ridge
18 Holes <> Par 71 <> Length 6839 yards <> $$
12930 Old Pumpkin Ridge Road - Cornelius, OR
503-647-9977 - Reservations Required
www.pumpkinridge.com

There are two 18-hole courses at Pumpkin Ridge, Ghost Creek and Witch Hollow; but Witch Hollow is only for members. The fairways on Ghost Creek weave their way through forests, and past wetlands and creeks. Designed for golfers of all levels, it has bent grass fairways, plenty of sand traps, and was designed to preserve the natural habitat for wildlife. Bob Cupp was the designer; this course opened in 1992 and quickly earned national recognition. With four sets of tees the slope ranges for 128 to 145, and the ratings from 69.2 to 74. Open year round from dawn to dusk. No denim on course; shirts must have collars.

Green fees are $50 November thru March for 18 holes, $150 June thru September, and $90 during April, May and October. After 1pm those rates drop to $30

November thru March; during the summer it drops to $90 at 3pm. In April, May and October you'll pay $60 after 2pm. Rental clubs are $45 a set, pull carts $8, and motorized carts are $16 per person when shared.

Facilities include a restaurant and lounge with a liquor license, plus banquet facilities, a full-service pro shop, 17-acre practice facility, 25-station driving range, chipping and putting greens, and practice bunkers. Lessons are available, as is help with tournament planning.

Directions: Take Highway 26 west of Portland to Dersham Road exit #55, go right to Mountaindale Road, turn right and follow this to Old Pumpkin Ridge Road and the course.

(Gresham)

Gresham Golf Course
18 Holes <> Par 72 <> Length 6043 yards <> $$
2155 NE Division - Gresham, OR
503-665-3352 - Reservations Required
www.greshamgolf.com

The Gresham Golf Course is open year round, is semi-flat, and has a nice view of Mt. Hood. Designed by Sam Wolsborn and Eddy Hogan, it opened in 1965 as a nine-hole course; the other nine were opened two years later. The slope is 111 and the rating 68.2. The women's par is 72 for a distance of 5849 yards. Hazards include a few shots over water, homes that edge more than half the holes, sand bunkers, and a small man-made lake.

Green fees on weekends and holidays are $18 for 9 holes or $31 for 18; the rest of the week you'll pay $16 and $28. Seniors can play 9 holes during the week for $12 and $23; on weekends and holidays seniors pay $14 and $27. Junior rates are $8 and $16 seven days a week. Power cart rental will add $7-16 per rider.

You'll find a covered driving range, putting and chipping greens, a restaurant and bar, banquet rooms, and a full-service pro shop. Lessons, and help with tournament planning, are available. At the driving range you'll pay $2.50 for 25 balls.

Directions: Located 12 miles east of downtown Portland, follow Division Avenue to Gresham.

(Hillsboro)

Killarney West Golf
9 Holes <> Par 36 <> Length 2544 yards <> $
1275 NW 334th - Hillsboro, OR
503-648-7634 - Reservations Advised

The fairways at Killarney West are narrow with lots of trees, two creeks, and a few small hills. Open year round, it is has bent grass greens and winter rye fairways. You'll find a water hole with a pond in the middle, lots of birds, and a quiet country setting. When the course is busy you are expected to move quickly, so slower golfers should go midweek. The slope is 108 and the course rating 64.4; the women's par is 37.

Green fees are $14 during the week and $18 on weekends and holidays. Clubs, handcarts, and motorized carts can all be rented. They have a putting green, chipping area, a small pro shop, and a snack bar with a liquor license.

Directions: Located on the west side of Hillsboro, right off Highway 8; take the exit for 334th and follow the signs.

McKay Creek Golf Course
9 Holes <> Par 36 <> Length 2761 yards <> $
1416 NW Jackson Street - Hillsboro, OR
503-693-7612 - Reservations Advised
www.mckaycreekgolf.com

McKay Creek was built on an old dairy farm; the original farmhouse serves as a clubhouse. Designed by Bill O'Meara and Jeremy Reding, it has winter rye fairways and bent grass greens. Opened in 1996, the slope is 103 and the course rating 64.8. From the ladies' tees the total distance is 2445 yards. This is a good place for beginners with three each par 3's, 4's, and 5's.

Green fees on weekends and holidays are $15 for 9 holes or $29 for 18. Monday thru Friday you'll pay $12 and $23; after 4pm those rates are $14 and $27. During the week juniors and seniors can play for $11 and $21 before 4pm. Carts rent for $12 and $23, pull carts $2, and clubs are $6 for a full set, $4 for a junior set.

Facilities include a 22-station lighted driving range and a full-service pro shop. Lessons are available. At the driving range you'll pay $3 for 25 balls, $7 for 65, or $9 for 105 balls.

Directions: Located at the western end of Hillsboro, just north of Highway 8.

Meriwether National Golf Course
36 Holes <> Par 72 <> Length 6719 yards <> $
5200 SW Rood Bridge Road - Hillsboro, OR
503-648-4143

Meriwether has three courses, the 18-hole **North Course**, 9-hole **South Course**, and the executive 9-hole **Short Course**. Fred Federspiel and Dave Powers are the designers.

The 18-hole North Course has some pretty difficult holes and borders the Tualatin River. You'll find a rolling terrain with trees, ponds and wildlife to keep the game interesting. Ten par 4's and 4 par 5's will make you work for that 72; the total distance is 6719 yards. The slope is 118 and the rating 70.9.

The 9-hole South Course is 3346 yards for a par of 36. This is an easy, flat course with just one water hazard. Greenside bunkers at every hole add challenge.

The Short Course is a challenging par 30; six par 3's and three par 4's make it quick. With a length of 1789 yards it's a good place to practice your short game. The water and trees require a true aim; from the yellow tees the distance is 1575 yards. This course rating is 57.8 and the slope 83.

Weekday green fees on the 9-hole and 18-hole courses, May thru early October, are $18 for 9 holes Monday thru Thursday, $20 the rest of the week. For 18 holes it will cost you $34 and $38. Winter rates for these two courses are $14-16 for 9 holes or $25-29 for 18. March thru April you'll pay $16-18 or $26-30 depending on whether it is a weekend or weekday. Juniors play for $8 and $15 year round.

On the Short Course green fees are $15 all week long May to October; $13 the rest of the year. Motorized carts rent for $16 and $28 in the summer, $14 and $26 the rest of the year. Pull carts rent for $3 year round.

They have a new clubhouse, restaurant/lounge with a liquor license, banquet room, covered driving range, full-service pro shop, snack bar, and chipping and putting greens. Lessons, and help with tournament planning, are available.

Directions: To find Meriwether, take Canyon Road west to the first stoplight past 239th, turn left onto Witch Hazel, go 1 mile to River Road, after 1 block turn left onto Rood Bridge, and follow this for 1 mile.

(Lake Oswego)

Lake Oswego Golf Course
18 Holes <> Par 54 <> Length 2538 yards <> $
17525 SW Stafford Road - Lake Oswego, OR
503-636-8228 - Reservations Advised
www.lakeoswegogolf.org

This well-groomed family course has some hills, a creek that winds past several holes, and first opened in 1970. Mount St. Helens and Mt. Hood can both be seen from the course.

Monday thru Thursday green fees March thru October are $14 for 9 holes or $23 for 18; Friday thru Sunday, and on holidays, they charge $16 and $26. Juniors and seniors can play 9 holes Monday thru Friday for $11, $16 on weekends; 18 holes are $18 and $26. They offer Twilight Specials Monday thru Thursday. Club and power cart rentals are available.

You'll find a restaurant, full-service pro shop, and a driving range with covered turf mats. At the range you can get a bucket of balls for $2.25 to $9, depending on how many you want. There is a sand practice area, and they offer lessons and help with tournament planning. The Bunkers Restaurant, located in the clubhouse, offers microbrews, a full wine list, and fine dining.

Directions: Take the Stafford exit off I-205, turn left, and drive 4 miles to the Lake Oswego Golf Course.

(Portland)

Broadmoor Golf Course
18 Holes <> Par 72 <> Length 6404 yards <> $
3509 NE Columbia Blvd - Portland, OR
503-281-1337 - Reservations Required
www.broadmoor-1931.com

This course was once a family dairy farm; in 1931 the six sisters who owned it had it turned into a golf course. This popular Portland course is busy; reservations are necessary March thru November. The course is very pleasant, and the terrain fairly flat with a few steep hills, lots of willow trees, lush greens, and a number of water holes. It is open year round, dawn to dusk, and has been in operation since 1931. The slope is 122 for men with a rating of 70.2; 110 and 69.9 for women. You can get reservations one week in advance.

Monday thru Friday you'll pay $15 for 9 holes or $28 for 18; weekend rates are $17 and $34. Play before 8am and you can get in on the early bird special – 18 holes for $15; they open at 6am. Seniors can play Monday thru Thursday, before 2pm, for $13 and $24; juniors can play any day of the week for $9 and $16. Power carts rent for $16 and $30 for two riders.

Facilities include a restaurant and lounge with a liquor license, plus banquet rooms, a snack bar, full service pro shop, and a driving range. They can provide help with tournament planning and offer lessons.

Directions: Leave I-5 at the Columbia Blvd. exit and head east 2 miles; from I-205 take the Columbia Blvd. exit 2 miles west.

Claremont Golf Course
9 Holes <> Par 36 <> Length 3077 yards <> $$
15955 NW West Union Road - Portland, OR
503-690-4589 - Reservations Recommended
www.claremontgolfclub.com

This year round course was built in 1989 and is easy to walk. It offers well-groomed fairways, nice greens, some challenging doglegs, and plenty of lakes and sand traps in a country-like setting. The first hole is a par three shot over water; the second hole is 554 yards for a par five.

June thru September, Friday thru Sunday and holiday rates are $18 for 9 holes or $30 for 18. During October it's $17-18 for 9 holes or $28-29 for 18, depending on the day of the week. November thru April it costs $16-17 for 9 holes or $28-29 for 18. Year round juniors and seniors pay $14 and $23 Friday thru Sunday and holidays, and $13 and $22 the rest of the week. Pull carts are $3-5 and power carts $12 per 9 holes for one.

Lessons are available, as well as snacks, beer, and wine. They can also provide help with tournament planning.

Directions: Take Highway 26 west to the 185th Avenue exit, turn right, and drive 1.5 miles.

Colwood National Golf Course
18 Holes <> Par 72 <> Length 6158 yards <> $$
7313 NE Columbia Blvd. - Portland, OR
503-254-5515 - Reservations Advised
www.colwoodgolfclub.com

This pleasant tree-lined course is fairly flat and open year round. The women's tees have a par of 74 for a total of 5974 yards. Foursomes need to call one week in advance if they want to play 18 holes.

Weekday green fees are $16 for 9 holes or $29 for 18 May thru September; weekend rates are $19 and $33. Juniors can play during the week for $9 and $17, or weekends for $13 and $24. Seniors can play Monday thru Friday before 11am for $13 and $23. Rates are lower off season. Clubs rent for $6 and $10, pull carts are $2-3, and motorized carts are $16 for 9 holes or $28 for 18.

The Colwood Bar and Grill is open 6:30am to dusk, and offers a great view of the golf course. They have banquet facilities, and a full-service pro shop where you can get help with tournament planning and arrange for lessons.

Directions: Located 18 blocks west of I-205 on Columbia Boulevard.

Eastmoreland Golf Course
18 Holes <> Par 71 <> Length 5864 yards <> $
2425 SE Bybee - Portland, OR
503-775-2900 - Reservations Advised
www.eastmorelandgolfcourse.com

Eastmoreland's terrain is very hilly, and the course is bordered by Crystal Springs Lake. This is one of the top courses in the United States, and has been the site of the city championship since 1918. Open year round, the women's par is 74 for a total distance of 5646 yards.

Friday thru Sunday, and on holidays, green fees are $21 for 9 holes or $37 for 18. Monday/Tuesday rates are $19 and $26; Wednesday/Thursday rates are $19 and $31. Seniors can play for $14 and $23 Monday thru Thursday, or $15 and $27 Friday thru Sunday. Juniors play for $9 and $14 Monday thru Thursday, $10 and $17 the rest of the week. Winter rates bring 9-hole fees down to $13 and $15, based on the day of the week.

Facilities include a restaurant and lounge with a liquor license and banquet facilities. You can get help with tournament planning and arrange for lessons at the full-service pro shop. They have a lighted two-story driving range that is open from dawn to 10pm during peak season. It has 34 tees, standing and brush mats, and a bucket of balls will cost you $3.75 to $9.75.

Directions: Leave Portland heading south on Highway 99E, take the exit marked Reed College, and cross over the highway.

Glendoveer Golf Course

36 Holes <> Par 73 <> Length 6296 yards <> $
14015 NE Glisan Street - Portland, OR
503-253-7507 - Reservations Advised
www.golfglendoveer.com

You'll find two 18-hole courses at Glendoveer, with ratings of 67.4 to 73.5. The greens are small and fast, the fairways tree lined, and the terrain hilly yet easy to walk. The designer is John Stenzel. The **West Course** is shorter than the **East Course**, with a total distance of 5922 yards for men and 5117 for women. Par for women is 75 on either course; on the West Course it's 71 for men, 73 on the East Course. The terrain is varied and heavily wooded.

Open year round, from daylight to dusk, reservations are necessary on the weekends. Springtime rates Monday thru Friday are $18 for 9 holes or $31 for 18; on weekends you'll pay $20 and $35. Seniors can play for $14 and $23 Monday thru Friday, $15 and $27 on Saturday and Sunday. Juniors pay $10 and $17 seven days a week and everyone can take advantage of the Twilight and Super Twilight specials when rates drop to $22 and $13 respectively.

Glendoveer has a great restaurant and lounge with a liquor license and banquet activities. They also have a snack bar, a double deck driving range, and a full-service pro shop where you can arrange for lessons and get help with tournament planning. The driving range has mat tees and is open year round. You can get a small bucket of balls for $3, medium for $5.50 or large for $8.

Directions: Located on Glisan Street, at 140th Street.

Heron Lakes Golf Course
36 Holes <> Par 72 <> Length 6615 yards <> $
3500 N Victory Blvd. - Portland, OR
503-289-1818 - Reservations Advised
www.heronlakesgolf.com

There are two 18-hole courses at Heron Lakes; **Green Back** and **Great Blue**. Both were designed by Robert Tent Jones Jr. and are open year round from sunup to sundown. Amenities include a restaurant that serves beer and wine, plus a full-service pro shop where lessons can be arranged, and a driving range with grass tees.

Heron Lakes' Green Back course has a flat terrain and is very easy to walk. The style is traditional with lots of trees and plenty of sand bunkers. The total distance is 6615 yards. This course has lots of water and a park-like setting. You'll find three tees at each hole; the slope is

113 to 124 and the ratings 69.4 to 71.4. Friday thru Sunday, as well as holidays, 18 holes will cost you $37; on Monday and Tuesday you'll pay $26, $31 on Wednesday and Thursday.

The Great Blue 18-hole course is very challenging and has a total distance of 6902 yards. It is Scottish-style, with rolling fairways, lots of water, and plenty of sand bunkers. With four tees at each hole, the slope is 140 and the course rating 73.2. Friday thru Sunday and on holidays, 18 holes will cost you $42; on Monday and Tuesday you'll pay $27, and it's $33 on Wednesday and Thursday.

Discounts are given to juniors and seniors for both 9-hole and 18-hole play. Early Bird and Twilight Specials lower the rates for everyone; Super Twilight rates are $13-15 all week long and begin 1.5 hours prior to sunset.

Directions: Leave I-5 at the Delta Park/Expo exit #306-B and go west to the course.

Portland Meadows Golf
9 Holes <> Par 31 <> Length 1983 yards <> $
901 N Schmeer Road - Portland, OR
503-289-3405 - Reservations Advised
www.portlandmeadows.com

Portland Meadows is a bargain course. Located on the infield of the Portland Meadows Race Track, it is only open May thru September. An easy-to-walk course, the women's par is 35. The slope is 84 and the course rating 29.7. Opened in 1961, it was designed by Eddie Hogan and Stan Terry.

On weekends and holidays green fees are $12 for 9 holes or $20 for 18; seniors pay $10 and $16. On Monday and Tuesday everyone plays for $9 and $15, and that price includes a free small bucket of balls at the driving range. Wednesday thru Friday rates are $9 and $18; $9 and $15 for seniors. Clubs rent for $6 and pull carts are $2.

Facilities include a limited pro shop where you can get help with tournament planning, and a snack bar offering cold beer. At the driving range you get a small bucket of balls for $3 or a large one for $5.

Directions: Take the Delta Park exit off I-5, turn right and follow this to the racetrack.

Rose City Golf Course
18 Holes <> Par 72 <> Length 6455 yards <> $
2200 NE 71st Avenue - Portland, OR
503-253-4744 - Reservations Advised

Rose City's setting is pretty, with lots of trees and water on the back nine. Open year round, this is the city's second oldest course. The slope is 118 and the rating 70.6. Three sets of tees add variety to the course. The women's par is 74 for a total distance of 5619 yards.

Weekend green fees are $20 for 9 holes or $35 for 18, seniors play for $15 and $27, and juniors for $10 and

$17. For 18 holes on Monday or Tuesday you'll pay $26, Wednesday/Thursday $29, and on Friday $31. Monday thru Friday everyone pays $18 for 9 holes, juniors pay $9 for 9 holes or $14 for 18, and seniors pay $14 and $23. During the winter you'll pay $13 and $19 during the week, or $15 and $25 on weekends.

Facilities include a full-service pro shop where you can get help with tournament planning and arrange for lessons. You'll find beer and wine at the snack bar.

Directions: The Rose City Golf Course is located just south of Halsey on 71st Avenue Northeast.

Wildwood Golf Course
18 Holes <> Par 72 <> Length 5756 yards <> $$
21881 SE St. Helens Road - Portland, OR
503-621-3402 - Reservations Advised
www.golfingwildwood.com

Designed by Bill O'Meara, and built in 1990, this course opened its second nine in 1996. You'll find lots of elevated tee shots and water on almost every hole. The fairways take you up and down gentle valleys where you'll find four small ponds and three creeks to challenge your game. You'll want a cart on this course; the slope is 113 and the course rating 68.3. Open year round, you can tee off at 8am during the week or 7am on weekends. The total distance from the women's tees is 4985 yards.

The sloping terrain, elevation changes, trees, bunkers, and water make this a challenging course. Green fees throughout the summer are $25 during the week and $30 on weekends to play 18 holes. During the winter you'll pay $22 and $28 for 18 holes.

Facilities include a snack bar where you will find cold beer, plus a full-service pro shop where you can get help with tournament planning and arrange for lessons. There is a limited driving range plus a chipping area.

Directions: Located on Hwy 30, 2 miles north of Cornelius Pass.

(Tigard)

Summerfield Golf Club
9 Holes <> Par 33 <> Length 2353 yards <> $
10650 SW Summerfield Drive - Tigard, OR
503-620-1200 - Reservations Needed

Summerfield is a semi-private course and closed to the public prior to 11am Tuesday thru Thursday, as well as Saturday mornings. Open year round, this executive course has a view of both Mt. Hood and Mount St. Helens. Designed by Ted Robinson Sr., the slope is 96 and the course rating 30.7; two sets of tees add variety. The ladies' tees have a total distance of 2231 yards.

Green fees are $10 per 9 holes on weekdays or $14 for 18 holes. They have no rental clubs, but handcarts can be rented for $2 and motorized carts are available as well. They also have a full-service pro shop where you can arrange for lessons.

Directions: Take I-5 south to the Carmen Drive exit, and follow this to Duram Road. The course is about 1.5 miles from the freeway.

(West Linn)

Sandelie 18-Hole Golf Course
27 Holes <> Par 70 <> Length 5894 yards <> $
28333 SW Mountain Road - West Linn, OR
503-655-1461 - Reservations Advised
www.sandeliegolfcouse.com

Sandelie has both an 18-hole and a 9-hole course; the 9-hole course is located in Wilsonville. The setting is quiet, and deer are often spotted on the fairways. Those fairways are partly wooded and one green is bordered by a pond; another is by a canyon, and the course terrain ranges from flat to gently rolling.

The **Sandelie East** Course is an 18-hole course with a slope of 99 and a course rating of 67.3. Open year round, from daylight to dusk.

During the week green fees are $13 for 9 holes, or $25 for 18. On weekend and holidays it will cost you $14 or

$27. Seniors can play on weekdays for $12 and $20. Clubs rent for $5 and handcarts are $2. Only a limited amount of golf carts are available. A snack bar and small pro shop are on site.

Directions: Leave I-205 at Stafford Road, head south 1 mile to Mountain Road, and turn left. The course is about 3 miles.

Roseburg

Myrtle Creek Golf Course
18 Holes <> Par 72 <> Length 6852 yards <> $$
1316 Fairway Drive - Myrtle Creek, OR
541-863-4653
www.myrtlecreekgolf.com

Undulating fairways, lots of trees, water, sand bunkers, and natural roughs make this a pretty and challenging course. Five sets of tees add variety; the distance from the red tees is only 4891 yards. Designed by Graham Cooke and Associates, the slope is 142 and the course rating 73.0; from the women's tees, 121 and 68.7.

Fall green fees are $30 if you're walking or $40 if you take a cart. Ten-play-punch-cards are available, keeping green fees $30 year round. Facilities include a year-round grass tee driving range, chipping and putting greens, and a pro shop where you can get help with individual and group lessons.

Directions: Located 18 miles southwest of Roseburg via I-5; take exit 108 to Myrtle Creek, go through the traffic light, over the bridge, and make a sharp left onto Riverside Drive. Turn right on Neal Lane and follow the signs to the golf course.

Stewart Park Golf Course
9 Holes <> Par 35 <> Length 2909 yards <> $
1005 Stewart Pkwy Drive - Roseburg, OR
541-672-4592 - Reservations Available

The Stewart Park course is flat with rolling hills, bent grass greens, and a variety of vegetation and wildlife. It was built in 1963, and is open year round, from dawn to dusk. Water hazards are found on four holes and there are enough trees to keep your aim sharp. From the men's tees the slope is 112 with a rating of 34.4. Par for women is 37 over a distance of 2778 yards.

During the week green fees are $14 and on weekends you'll pay $16. Facilities include practice areas, a restaurant where beer and wine is available, plus a full-service pro shop and a driving range. Lessons, and help with tournament planning, are available.

Directions: Leave I-5 at the Stewart Parkway exit and head west.

Salem

Auburn Center Golf

9 Holes <> Par 29 <> Length 1338 yards <> $
5220 Center Street NE - Salem, OR
503-363-4404

Auburn center Golf is only closed on Christmas Day. Opened in 1959, it has flat, tree-lined fairways that present a challenge to even the most accurate golfer. It is also one of the most reasonably priced courses around, and was built on the site of an old apple orchard. The fairways are winter rye and the greens bent grass.

Seven days a week green fees are $11 for 9 holes. Facilities include a snack bar, limited pro shop, and a miniature golf course.

Directions: Take the Market Street exit off I-5, head east to Lancaster, go south (right) to Center Street, and east (left) 1.5 miles to the course.

Cottonwood Lakes Golf

9 Holes <> Par 28 <> Length 1148 yards <> $
3225 River Road S - Salem, OR
503-364-3673

Built in 1991, this year-round course is open 8am to dusk during the week, and 7am to dusk on weekends. The greens are bent grass and the fairways winter rye; it is a flat, easy to walk course. You'll find lots of water, plenty of trees, and two sets of tees.

This is another bargain course; you'll pay $14 for 9 holes seven days a week. Rental equipment is not available. Both individual and group lessons are available.

Directions: Leave South Commercial on Owen, which soon becomes River Road, and follow this for 2 miles to the course.

Creekside Golf Club
18 Holes <> Par 72 <> Length 6887 yards <> $$$
6250 Clubhouse Drive SE - Salem, OR
503-363-4653 - Reservations Advised
www.golfcreekside.com

This semi-private course has over 100 bunkers, water on 12 holes, and mature trees. The 16th hole requires golfers to shoot the ball through a narrow opening in a stand of Douglas fir. Designed by Peter Jacobsen, it opened in late 1993. The slope is 134 and the course rating 71.4, the terrain is gently rolling, and five sets of tees are available. The total distance from the ladies' tees is 5167 yards. They open at 6am on weekends and 7am during the week.

Green fees are $40 for 18 holes; for $55 a cart is included. Facilities include a big clubhouse with banquet facilities, a restaurant overlooking the lake and 9th green, a snack bar serving cold beer, plus a full-service pro shop and driving range. Lessons are available.

Directions: Leave I-5 at the Kuebler exit, head west to Sunnyside, and go south 1 mile to the course.

McNary Golf Club
18 Holes <> Par 71 <> Length 6215 yards <> $$
6255 River Road N - Salem, OR
503-393-4653 - Reservations Advised
www.mcnarygolfclub.com

McNary is flat with elevated greens. A semi-private course, it has been in existence since 1962. You'll find several lakes, a creek, and a growing number of sand traps to keep your aim sharp. It also offers a nice view of Mt. Hood when the skies are clear; the slope is 121 and the course rating 69.2. A creek comes into play on 4 holes. Open year round, the women's par is 71 for a total distance of 5325 yards.

You'll pay $28 for 9 holes or $50 for 18 on weekends, $26 and $44 on weekdays, April thru October. Twilight rates begin at 2pm and fees are $17 for 9 holes or $34 for 18. Seniors can play 18 holes during the week for $35. Power carts rent for $18 and $28 and pull carts are $3.

Facilities include a restaurant and lounge with a liquor license, banquet facilities that will seat 200, a full service pro shop, and practice greens. Help with lessons, and tournament planning, are available.

Directions: McNary is 5 miles north of Salem, 1 mile west of I-5.

Meadowlawn Golf Course
9 Holes <> Par 32 <> Length 2043 yards <> $
3898 Meadowlawn Loop SE - Salem, OR
503-363-7391 - Reservations Advised
www.meadowlawngolf.net

Meadowlawn was once a dairy farm and is not as easy as it looks. The terrain is flat with elevated greens, and the course is fairly fast during the summer. Open 7am to 6pm year round, hazards include trees and water.

Green fees during the week are $16 for 9 holes or $28 for 18. On weekends you'll pay $18 and $30. Juniors can play 9 holes for $12 and $20 for 18 all week long. Seniors, age 60 and over, play for $15 and 27. Active duty military rates are $12 for 9 holes any day of the week. Power carts rent for $13 and $22.

Facilities include a full-service pro shop and a snack bar. Beer and wine is available, and you can arrange for lessons and get help with tournament planning.

Directions: Take the Market Street exit off I-5 and head down Lancaster. Go past State Street and after the road curves turn at the second light and follow the signs.

Salem Golf Club
18 Holes <> Par 72 <> Length 6200 yards <> $$
2025 Golf Course Road S - Salem, OR
503-363-6652 - Reservations Advised
www.salemgolfclub.com

The Salem Golf Club course opened in 1928, and is the oldest in the city. A semi-private club, it has gently rolling hills and is easy to walk. This course has lots of trees and many large pines; three sets of tees give it variety. The slope is 118 and the ratings 69.6 for men, 72.9 for women. The course is open year round.

Green fees are $28 for 9 holes or $50 for 18 all week long. Twilight rates begin at 3pm when everyone pays $30 for 18 holes; the discount begins at 4:30pm for 9 holes, it's just $28. Juniors play after 1pm on weekends for $10 and $20. Motorized carts rent for $12 and $24, pull carts are $2, and clubs can be rented for $10.

They have a restaurant and lounge with a liquor license and banquet room, plus a snack bar, full-service pro shop, and driving range. Lessons, and help with tournament planning, are available. At the driving range you can get 50 balls for $5, 100 for $8, or 150 for $10.

Directions: Located 2 miles from downtown Salem via South River Road.

Sutherlin

Sutherlin Knolls Golf Course
18 Holes <> Par 72 <> Length 6325 yards <> $
1919 Recreation Lane - Sutherlin, OR
541-459-4422 - Reservations Advised

Sutherlin Knolls is in a beautiful country setting. It has rolling hills, wooded areas, and wildlife. It's a challenging older course with many new features and continual upgrades. They are open year round from daylight to dusk. Water hazards come into play on seven holes, and the women's par is 75 for a total distance of 5636 yards.

Green fees are $14 for 9 holes or $22 for 18 during the week, $15 and $25 on weekends. Golf clubs, pull carts, and motorized carts can all be rented. Facilities include a restaurant and lounge with a liquor license, plus a banquet room, pro shop, and driving range.

Directions: Leave I-5 at exit #36 and head west on 138th; you can follow the signs from there.

Umpqua Golf Resort
18 Holes <> Par 72 <> Length 6491 yards <> $$
1919 Recreation Lane - Sutherlin, OR
541-459-4422
www.umpquagolfresort.com

The Umpqua Golf Resort sits on the site of the old Oak Hills Golf Club, and has been wonderfully transformed. Six all new holes were added. Rolling hills, the natural terrain, lakes, and streams make this a pretty and challenging course.

Weekday green fees are $18 for 9 holes or $29 for 18; on the weekend you'll pay $20 and $35. Juniors pay $8 and $10 during the week, $10 and $15 on weekends.

Motorized carts are $10 per person on weekdays and $15 per person on the weekends.

Facilities include a covered driving range and a pro shop where you can get help with lessons and tournament planning. There is also a 41 space RV park with full hookups.

Directions: Located just west of I-5 along Highway 138.

Vernonia

Vernonia Golf Club
18 Holes <> Par 71 <> Length 5536 yards <> $
15961 Timber Road E - Vernonia, OR
503-429-6811 - Reservations Advised

The Vernonia Golf Club course is nestled in timber, along the Nehalem River. It's quiet, beautiful, and a pleasure to play, but if your ball leaves the course, it's gone. The drainage is excellent, so the greens are dry when other courses are too wet to play. You'll find a few hills, but the course is easy to walk. The slope is 113 and the rating 66.8. This course is open year round from dawn to dusk. The front nine were built in 1926; the back nine opened in 1999.

Weekend green fees are $15 for 9 holes of $25 for 18. On weekdays it's $10 and $20. Seniors play for $12 and

$22. Facilities include a snack bar where you'll find cold beer and wine, plus a banquet room, and a full-service pro shop. Lessons, and help with tournament planning, are available.

Directions: Vernonia is located northwest of Portland via Highways 26 and 47. At Vernonia turn left on Timber Road and follow this to the course.

Warren

St. Helens Golf Course
9 Holes <> Par 36 <> Length 2977 yards <> $
57246 Hazen Road - Warren, OR
503-397-0358
www.sthelensgolfcourse.com

This course offers a beautiful view of Mount St. Helens, Mt. Hood and Mt. Adams. The terrain is flat and the course is open year round. Built in 1959, it offers two sets of tees for those looking to play 18 holes. The women's tees have a total distance of 2985 yards. The slope is 114 and the course rating 68.1.

Weekday green fees are $14 for 9 holes or $25 for 18; on weekends you'll pay $16 and $30. Clubs rent for $5, handcarts $2, and motorized carts are $12 per 9 holes.

They have a practice area, chipping and putting greens, a full-service pro shop, banquet facilities, and a snack bar where beer is available. Lessons, and help with tournament planning, can be arranged. A new state-of-the-art warm-up hitting cage has been added.

Directions: Warren is located a half mile south of St. Helens. To find the course leave Highway 30 on Church Road, drive 2 miles to Hazen Road, and turn right.

Welches

The Resort at the Mountain
27 Holes <> Par 36 <> Length 3092 yards <> $$
68010 E Fairway Avenue - Welches, OR
800-669-4653 - Reservations Required
www.theresort.com

You'll find the Resort at the Mountain in a scenic valley at the edge of the Mt. Hood National Forest Wilderness Area. It includes three 9-hole courses with a Scottish theme and greens that are among the finest in the Northwest. The scenery is spectacular and the terrain includes hills, meadows, ponds, creeks and rivers.

The **Pine Cone** course was built in 1928, and is probably the most scenic. **Thistle** was built in 1966 and **Foxglove** in 1980. All three are open year round, weather permitting, and are mostly flat with at least one hill. The shortest course is 2681 yards for a par of 34, the longest 3351 yards with a par of 36.

Green fees during the summer are $25 for 9 holes or $50 for 18. During October, and January thru April, you'll pay $20 and $40. In November and December rates are $18 and $35; in May you'll pay $50 for 18 holes. Juniors play for $16 and $32 all week long. Carts rent for $9 and $15 per person, and clubs are $15-45, depending on the quality of the set.

Family golf rates Sunday through Friday, between 3:30 and 5pm, are $25 per adult with one child per adult playing for free. Clubs are available on a first-come basis for $5. The 18-hole putting course, also known as The Greens, charges $8 for adults and $5 for kids.

This luxury resort has a fine restaurant, liquor license, a complete conference center, full-service pro shop, tennis courts, and a fitness center. Lessons are available.

Directions: Located 40 miles east of Portland via Highway 26.

Wilsonville

Charbonneau Golf Course
27 Holes <> Par 31 <> Length 2148 yards <> $$

2020 Charbonneau Drive - Wilsonville, OR
503-694-1246 - Reservations Advised

You'll find three nine-hole courses at Charbonneau. Each has a par of 31 and three sets of tees. The total distance on the **North Nine** is 2113, the **West Nine** is 2007, and the **East Nine** is 2148. Located south of Portland, this flat course has a nice view of Mt. Hood and is open year round.

Weekday green fees are $17 for 9 holes or $26 for 18. On weekends and holidays they charge $18 and $30. Clubs rent for $8 and $15, handcarts $4 and $6, and motorized carts $8 and $12 per person.

Facilities include a driving range and a full-service pro shop where you can arrange for lessons and get help with tournament planning.

Directions: Leave I-5 at exit #282B, turn left, and follow the signs.

Sandelie West 9 Golf Course
9 Holes <> Par 70 <> Length 5894 yards <> $
3030 SW Advance Road - Wilsonville, OR
503-682-2022
www.sandeliegolfcourse.com

Sandelie in West Linn has opened this 9-hole course in nearby Wilsonville. It is open from early spring through mid fall, Tuesday thru Sunday. It's a pretty straight-forward course with three sets of tees, open fairways, and old growth trees. Wildlife is often seen on the course. This is a good place for beginners, and it's nice and quiet.

Green fees are $14 for 9 holes or $27 for 18 on weekends and holidays; $13 and $25 during the week. Juniors and seniors can play Monday thru Friday for $12 and $20. Pull carts rent for $2 and clubs for $5.

Directions: From I-5 take the Wilsonville exit #283 and head east for 1.7 miles. The course is on the right side of the road.

Woodburn

Tukwila OGA Member's Course
18 Holes <> Par 72 <> Length 6565 yards <> $$$
2850 Hazelnut Drive - Woodburn, OR
503-981-4653 - Reservations Advised
www.ogagolfcourse.com

The first nine holes at Tukwila opened in late 1994, the second nine in 1996. Designed by Bill Robinson, this year round course operates dawn to dusk. The terrain is flat and easy to walk with some mounding. It contains several lakes, natural wetlands, a filbert orchard, and mature evergreens. Four sets of tees are available; the slope is 132 and the course rating 71.4.

Non-member green fees are $40 on weekdays and $45 on weekends. Golf clubs, pull carts, and motorized carts are available for rental. Facilities include a member clubhouse with cold beer, plus a golf museum, full-service pro shop, 12,000-square-foot putting course, and a driving range. Help with tournament planning, and lessons, are available.

Directions: Leave I-5 at the Woodburn exit, turn left, go 1 mile to Boones Ferry Road, turn left again, and follow the signs.

Region Three

Central Oregon

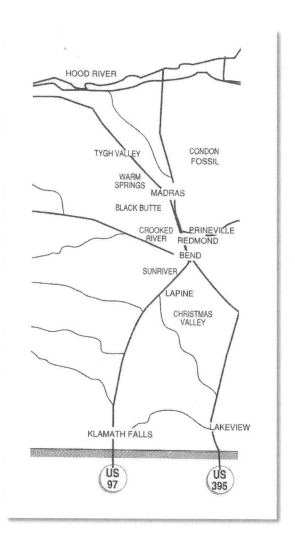

COURSES IN CENTRAL OREGON

Central Oregon is a golfer's haven, with deluxe golf resorts and lots of new courses. This region includes the east side of the Cascade Mountains; some areas get sunshine close to 300 days a year making it a good place to escape the wet Willamette Valley.

The mountain views are gorgeous, and the towns small enough to enjoy. Sunriver, Kah-Nee-Ta, Crooked River Ranch, and the Bend area are all great vacation destinations for golfers.

The natural desert landscape and lava outcroppings found here will provide challenge to anyone looking to perfect their game. These courses will have you shooting across a river gorge, through a series of small ponds, onto an island green, and past lots of sand.

Central Oregon golf course designers include Jack Nicklaus, Tom Fazio, Bunny Mason, John Thronson, Robert Muir Graves, Robert Cupp, Robert Trent Jones II and Fred Federspiel to name a few.

The following cities in Central Oregon have golf courses.

Bend	Fossil
Black Butte	Hood River
Christmas Valley	Klamath Falls
Condon	Lakeview
Crooked River	LaPine

Madras   Sunriver
Prineville   Tygh Valley
Redmond   Warm Springs
Sisters

Bend

Lost Tracks Golf Club
18 Holes <> Par 72 <> Length 7000 yards <> $$
60205 Sunset View Drive - Bend, OR
541-385-1818

Lost Tracks has a rolling terrain and was designed by Brian Whitcomb. It's a challenging course with fantastic views, plenty of water, and lots of sand. On the 16th hole you have a big island green, surrounded by water and sand; the 9th hole has a dogleg that will sharpen your skills. The course slope is 124 from the green tees, 123 from the blue tees, and from the women's tees it's 127. Ratings are 71.8, 68.5, and 69.7 for those tees.

Green fees during peak season, mid June thru September, are $37 for 9 holes and $61 for 18, Monday thru Thursday. Friday thru Sunday 18 holes goes up to $72. Off season rates are $27-32 for 9 holes and $40-50 for 18. Motorized carts add $7-15 to the total per person rate.

Twilight rates begin at 3pm and will cost you $35-40 depending on the time of year. Juniors can play 9 holes for $20 or 18 for $30; add $5 per 9 holes for a cart. Facilities include a full service pro shop and restaurant. Group and private lessons are available.

Directions: Located south of Bend; follow US 97 south to the Baker Road exit, #143, toward Knott Road. After .3 mile turn left onto Baker Road and stay straight when it becomes Knott Road; follow this 1.3 miles to China Hat Road, turn right, then right again onto Sunset View Drive. The course is 1.3 miles.

Mountain High Golf Course
9 Holes <> Par 36 <> Length 2882 yards <> $$
60650 China Hat Road - Bend, OR
541-382-1111 - Reservations Available

Mountain High is open April thru October. Built in 1987, this was once an 18-hole course; what remains is the back nine. The Old Back Nine is a level tree-lined course where you'll find three sets of tees; and you get a great mountain view. Course hours are 7am to dusk.

Green fees are $20 for 9 holes or $36 for 18 all week long. Clubs rent for $10, handcarts $2, and motorized carts $10 per 9 holes. Facilities include a practice green, a snack bar where you can get a cold beer, and a small pro shop.

Directions: Leave Bend heading south on Highway 97 and turn east on China Hat Road. The course is .5 mile.

River's Edge Golf Course
18 Holes <> Par 72 <> Length 6683 yards <> $$
400 Pro Shop Drive - Bend, OR
541-389-3111 - Reservations Advised
www.riverhouse.com

Located between the Deschutes River and Awbrey Butte, River's Edge was designed by Robert Muir Graves and opened in 1988. The second nine was finished in 1992. It has a number of small hills and valleys, and some excellent views.

There's a waterfall feeding a lake in front of the 5th hole and a 100 foot drop in elevation on the 15th. The slope is 137 and the ratings 72.4 for men, and 71.2 for women with a slope of 133. Four tees are available on each hole. Weather permitting, the course is open year round. The women's par is 73 for a total distance of 5340 yards.

Green fees during the summer are $37 for 9 holes or $59 for 18; winter rates are $23 and $39. Junior discounts are available. Twilight rates are $39 in the summer and $30 the balance of the year. You can rent pull carts for $5 and $7, and motorized carts are $10 and $16; club rentals are available as well.

They have a fine dining restaurant, plus Bogey's Cafe, a place where golfers will find food and drinks plus a deck overlooking the course.

At the pro shop you'll find help with tournament planning and lessons. They also have a driving range with grass tees and distance targets. Putting green and practice facility are available.

Directions: Take Mt. Washington Drive off Highway 97 and follow the signs.

Tetherow Golf Club
18 Holes <> Par 72 <> Length 7298 yards <> $$$$$
61240 Skyline Ranch Road - Bend, OR
541-388-2582
www.tetherow.com

The public is welcome at Tetherow except between 12:20 and 1:40pm; the course opens to the public at 9:40am. Open April thru October, you'll find five sets of tees; the shortest distance is 5342 yards, the longest 7298. They have a strict dress code here; denim is not allowed and shirts must be collared.

Designed by David McLay Kidd, this links-style course has lots of bunkers, knobs, and knolls. The views are gorgeous; you can see the Cascade Mountains from this high desert course.

Non-members are required to hire a forecaddie; the cost is included in the green fees, tipping is expected. You'll pay $175 for 18 holes or $135 for 9 holes June thru September. Off-season rates range from $85 to $119. Replay is just $40. Rental clubs include TaylorMade and Nike; the cost is $40.

Facilities include The Tetherow Grill Restaurant and Bar, as well as deluxe accommodations, and a pro shop.

Directions: Follow SW Century Drive to Skyline Ranch Road and turn right.

Widgi Creek Golf Club
18 Holes <> Par 72 <> Length 6911 yards <> $$
18707 Century Drive - Bend, OR
541-382-4449

This Robert Muir Graves course opened in 1990. It has undulating greens, narrow fairways, plus lots of trees, lakes and bunkers to challenge your game, and four tees per hole. The slope is 134 with a rating of 73.4; from the ladies' tees the total distance is 5070 yards. This semi-private course is open to the public from 10am to 4pm. Widgi Creek is closed November thru February. The rest of the year reservations are available two weeks in advance.

Green fees during peak season are $50 for 9 holes or $75 for 18. Off-season rates drop as low as $29; juniors pay $25 for 9 holes or $29 for 18 whenever they're open. Pull carts rent for $5 and motorized carts are $11-16, depending on the season.

Facilities include a restaurant/lounge with a liquor license, plus a banquet room, snack bar, full-service pro shop, large practice green, and a driving range. At the range you'll find grass tees and you can get a bucket of balls for $5. Lessons, and help with tournament planning, are available.

Directions: Take Cascade Lakes Highway toward Mt. Bachelor; the course is just a five minute drive out of Bend.

Black Butte

Black Butte Ranch Course
36 Holes <> Par 72 <> Length 7002 yards <> $$$
Black Butte Ranch - Black Butte, OR
541-595-1270
www.blackbutteranch.com

You'll find two 18-hole golf courses at Black Butte. Carved out of the forest and open April thru October, these courses have a beautiful view of snow-capped mountains. Aspen and pine trees provide natural hazards; the sand bunkers will also challenge your shot.

The **Big Meadow** course was designed by Robert Muir Graves and has lots of beautiful mountain views. It is easy to walk and the women's total distance is 5485 yards. The **Glaze Meadow** course will reopen in 2012, once the renovations are complete. The total yardage on that course is 7079 for a par of 72. The redesign was headed by John Fought.

From May 27th thru September you'll pay $39 for 9 holes or $73 for 18. Spring and fall rates are $33 and $59. Twilight rates start at 3pm and everyone pays $53 for 18 holes. They rent clubs for $18 and $30, pull carts for $3 and $5, and motorized carts are $20 and $32.

Each course has its own driving range and pro shop, where lessons can be arranged. Facilities include a restaurant and lounge with a liquor license, plus meeting rooms and overnight accommodations. If you plan to stay at Black Butte Ranch, ask about their golf packages.

Directions: Black Butte Ranch is located 9 miles northwest of Sisters, at the foot of Black Butte.

Christmas Valley

Christmas Valley Golf Course
9 Holes <> Par 36 <> Length 3393 yards <> $
#1 Christmas Tree Lane - Christmas Valley, OR
541-576-2216
www.cvgolfcourse.org

The terrain at Christmas Valley is flat with raised greens and tee boxes. Built in 1964, the course is open year round; the slope is 118 and the course rating 35.0. The women's tees have a par of 38 for a total distance of 3070 yards. Roughs consist of sagebrush, wild desert grasses and sand; there's a water hazard on the 9th hole with resident geese.

Green fees are $15 for 9 holes or $20 for 18 year round; annual memberships are available for $175, family memberships for $225. When golfing off season, bring exact change and deposit the required amount in the honor box. This course is known for pasture-style golf; the layout is flat and narrow.

Facilities include a restaurant and lounge next door with a liquor license.

Directions: The course is easy to reach from downtown Christmas Valley; just follow the signs to Christmas Tree Lane.

Condon

Condon Municipal Golf Course
9 Holes <> Par 36 <> Length 3131 yards <> $
515 N Lincoln - Condon, OR
541-384-4266
www.cityofcondon.com

The Condon Municipal Golf Course is open year round. The terrain is slightly rolling, yet flat and easy to walk. It's a challenging little course with long narrow fairways.

The slope is 112 and the course rating 69.4. This is a good course to practice those windy shots.

You can play all day long for $15 or play 9 holes for $10. Students, families, and individuals can buy annual passes for reduced rates. Pull carts rent for $1 when the course is staffed.

Directions: Located at the north end of town.

Crooked River

Crooked River Ranch Course
18 Holes <> Par 71 <> Length 5661 yards <> $$
5195 Club House Road - Crooked River, OR
541-923-6343 - Reservations Advised
www.crookedriverranch.com

The Crooked River course provides a challenge for golfers of all levels. From the 3rd tee you have a terrific view of the 300 foot deep Crooked River Gorge; on the 5th hole you play across it, shooting along the curve of the river.

The slope is 107 and the ratings 66.3 for men, 67.2 for women. A year-round course, it has rolling hills with juniper, sagebrush and rocks lining the fairways. The second nine was added in 1994 and designed by Jim Ramey.

Summer weekday green fees are $23 for 9 holes or $41 for 18. On weekends and holidays prior to noon you'll pay $28 and $48; 18 holes are $44 after 12pm. Monday thru Thursday seniors play for $21 and $36. During March, April and October weekend rates are $23 for 9 holes or $40 for 18; Monday thru Friday you'll pay $21 and $36. In October seniors play for $18 and $36. Clubs rent for $12 and $20, pull carts are $3-4, and motorized cart rates are based on the number of riders and holes.

Amenities include a nice restaurant and lounge, banquet facilities, a driving range, pro shop, RV park, and tennis courts. At the pro shop you can get help with tournament planning and arrange for lessons. On the driving range you'll pay $7 for a bucket of balls; ask for a free bucket of balls when you pay your green fees.

Directions: Take Highway 97 north of Redmond 5 miles to Lower Bridge Road West and follow the signs.

Fossil

Kinzua Hills Golf Club
6 Holes <> Par 22 <> Length 3033 yards <> $
Kinzua Road - Fossil, OR
541-763-3287

Although Kinzua Hills has only 6 holes, you can use the two sets of tees to play a full 18 with some variety. The par for 18 holes is 65. Built in 1929, the slope is 89 and the course rating 29.9. You can generally play this course from early May until mid-September.

Kinzua Hills operates on the honor system, so bring correct change. You can play 6 holes for $5, 12 for $10, or 18 for $15. You'll find a lock box on the club house porch. When the clubhouse is open you can rent clubs, handcarts, and motorized carts.

Directions: Located 9 miles southeast of Fossil. Leave Highway 19 about 3 miles south of town; take Kinzua Road east 5 miles to the course.

Hood River

Hood River Golf
18 Holes <> Par 71 <> Length 6109 yards <> $
1860 Country Club Road - Hood River, OR
541-386-3009 - Reservations Advised
www.hoodrivergolf.net

Hood River is one of the prettiest courses in the state; you get outstanding views of Mt. Adams, Mt. Hood and the Hood River Valley from the fairways. This course first opened in 1922 and only closes during heavy snows.

The terrain is varied, with some hills, and you can choose from four sets of tees for variety. In 1999 the back nine was added; the terrain there is very hilly.

Daily green fees are $16 for 9 holes or $30 for 18; seniors can play for $12 and $22. On Wednesdays everyone plays 9 holes for $10 or 18 for $20. And, if you're older than 80 you can golf for free.

Facilities include a pitching and chipping area, practice green, driving range, and a bar and grill with banquet facilities. Hood River has a full-service pro shop where you can arrange for lessons, shop, and get help with tournament planning.

Directions: Take I-84 to exit #62, head toward West Hood River, turn right on Country Club Road, and go 4.5 miles.

Indian Creek Golf Course
18 Holes <> Par 72 <> Length 6150 yards <> $
3605 Brookside Drive - Hood River, OR
541-386-7770

There's a view of Mt. Hood or Mt. Adams from every hole at Indian Creek. The greens are smooth and true rolling; the fairways are lined with trees and water. Open year round, the slope is 129 with a rating of 71.3. The total distance from the women's tees is 4547 yards.

Monday thru Thursday green fees April thru September are $21 for 9 holes or $39 for 18. The rest of the week, and on holidays, you'll pay $25 and $49. November thru February you'll pay $14 and $25 Monday thru Thursday, or $18 and $32 the balance of the year. You can rent clubs for $15-35, pull carts are $6, and motorized carts $20 for 9 holes or $30 for 18.

Facilities include a full-service pro shop, driving range, and a snack bar where you'll find cold beer. They provide help with tournament planning and lessons. At the driving range you'll pay $4-8 for a bucket of balls.

Directions: Leave I-84 on exit #62 and head east on Cascade, turn right onto 13th Street, and right on Brookside.

Klamath Falls

Harbor Links Golf Course
18 Holes <> Par 71 <> Length 6132 yards <> $$
601 Harbor Isles Blvd. - Klamath Falls, OR
541-882-0609 - Reservations Available
www.harborlinksgolf.net

You'll find lots of water at the Harbor Links course. Built in 1985, it's open year round and they take reservations one week in advance. The course is very easy to walk and has a links-style construction.

Daily green fees are $28 for 9 holes or $55 for 18; seniors can play for $24 and $45. Juniors, age 17 and younger, pay $9 per 9 holes. Clubs rents for $9-12, pull carts $3-5, and motorized carts are $15 and $28.

Facilities include chipping and putting greens, a restaurant and lounge, plus a full-service pro shop and driving range. Lessons, and help with tournament planning, are available. The range has mat tees and you can get a bucket of balls for $3-9.

Directions: Located north of the yacht club, along Klamath Lake.

Round Lake Golf Course
9 Holes <> Par 30 <> Length 1512 yards <> $
4000 Round Lake Road - Klamath Falls, OR
541-884-2520
www.roundlakerv.com

This scenic executive course is surrounded by pine trees and mountains. Open from the middle of March through the middle of November, it's generally easy to get a walk-on tee time. This is a flat course with some water and wildlife.

Green fees at Round Lake are extremely reasonable. Any day of the week you can play 9 holes for $9 or 18 for $15. Electric golf carts are $7 for 9 holes or $12 for 18.

Facilities include a pro shop where you'll find snacks and drinks, and a driving range. At the driving range you can get a bucket of balls for $3.50.

Directions: Head west 4.4 miles on Highway 66 to Round Lake Road; turn right and go 3.6 miles to Round Lake Estates and the course.

Running Y Ranch Golf Course
18 Holes <> Par 72 <> Length 7138 yards <> $$$$
5000 Running Y Road - Klamath Falls, OR
800-569-0029 - Reservations Required
www.runningy.com

This is the only Arnold Palmer designed golf course in Oregon, and it's quite pretty. Water and sand, rocks and roughs, all add to the challenge. From the ladies' tees the total distance is 5365 yards. The course slope is 132 and the total distance 73.4 yards; four sets of tees add real variety to the game. There is also an 18-hole putting course at this location, complete with water hazards and sand traps. It's great fun for families.

Green fees on the 18-hole Palmer course for non-guests, May thru September, are $55 for 9 holes or $99 for 18 all week long. Junior rates are $16 for 9 holes or $30 for 18. Clubs rent for $20 per 9 holes and pull carts are $2. On the putting course adults pay $10 and those younger than 18 pay $5. Putters are included on the mini-course.

Facilities include deluxe resort accommodations, a restaurant and lounge, pro shop, and lots of local recreation.

Directions: Take Highway 140W off Lakeshore Drive. Drive .9 mile to Running Y Road; it's .4 mile from there.

Shield Crest Golf Course
18 Holes <> Par 72 <> Length 7005 yards <> $$
3151 Shield Crest Drive - Klamath Falls, OR
541-884-1493 - Reservations Available
www.shieldcrestgc.com

Shield Crest offers terrific views of Mt. Shasta from almost anywhere on the course. Open year round, it was built in 1989, and operates from sunrise to sunset. You'll find only a few hills on this fairly flat course, and three tees at every hole. The women's par is 74 for a total distance of 6318 yards.

Green fees are $25 for 9 holes or $35 for 18 if you're walking; $35 and $50 if you need a cart. On Tuesdays and Thursdays after 2pm two golfers can play for $25.

They have a restaurant and lounge where liquor is served, plus a driving range, and a full-service pro shop. Lessons, and help with tournament planning, are available.

Directions: Located 2 miles east of Highway 140's Lakeview Junction.

Lakeview

Lakeridge Golf & Country Club
9 Holes <> Par 36 <> Length 3324 yards <> $
94378 Highway 140 - Lakeview, OR
541-947-3855

Weather permitting, Lakeridge is open year round. This is a long, flat course with a pond on the 9th hole and lots of sand traps. Tee times are not necessary, but you might want to call ahead to be sure the course is not closed for a tournament, especially during late June and early July. The women's par is 37 for a total distance of 2898 yards; the slope is 121 and the course rating 35.9.

Green fees are $14 for 9 holes or $26 for 18 all week long. Clubs rent for $3-4, pull carts are $3-4, and motorized carts $15 for 9 holes or $25 for 18.

They have a full-service pro shop, driving range, and a restaurant with banquet facilities and a liquor license. At the driving range you can get a bucket of balls for $3. They can also help you with golf lessons as well as tournament planning.

Directions: Located 4 miles west of Lakeview on Highway 140.

LaPine

Quail Run Golf Course
18 Holes <> Par 36 <> Length 6800 yards <> $$
16725 Northridge Drive - LaPine, OR
541-536-1303 - Reservations Advised

The fairways at Quail Run are carved out of the woods, and each one is separated by acres of trees. The course was designed by Jim Ramey and opened in 1991. It has four tees per hole, a rolling terrain, water hazards, and white sand bunkers that present a challenge to golfers of all levels.

The slope is 126 with a rating of 72.2 for men; the slope is 116 and the rating 69.6 for women. From the women's tees the total distance is 5400 yards. Open February thru December, weather permitting. As you play, you'll find some great mountain views, and come upon a couple of super Mt. Bachelor viewpoints.

You can play 9 holes at Quail Run for $35 or 18 for $55 between May 28 and the end of September. Off-season rates are $25 and $42. Motorized carts are $7.50 for 9 holes or $13 for 18. Twilight rates begin at 2pm during peak season, 1pm off season; this is when 9-hole rates are charged for 18 holes of play.

Amenities include a restaurant offering cold beer and wine, plus a driving range, and full-service pro shop. Lessons, and tournament planning assistance, are

THE NORTHWEST GOLFER: OREGON EDITION

available. At the driving range you'll find grass tees and get a bucket of balls for $4-6.

Directions: Take Highway 97 south of Sunriver 9 miles to the East Lake/Paulina junction and go 2 miles west.

Madras

Desert Peaks Golf Club
9 Holes <> Par 36 <> Length 3231 yards <> $
565 NW Adler <> Madras, OR
541-475-6368
www.desertpeaksgolf.com

This city course has lots of wide open space and nice mountain views. The total distance from the red tees is 2767 yards. The course rating is 67.2 and the slope 110.

Green fees during the week are $10 for 9 holes or $17 for 18; on weekends and holiday you'll pay $12 and $20. During the week juniors can play for $7 and $12. Punch cards bring the cost of 9 holes down to $9 a game, and on Mondays you can bring and friend and both play 9 holes for $15. Clubs rent for $6 and $10, pull carts $2 and $3, and motorized carts are $10 and $20. If you bring your own cart the trail fee is $5 and $8. Memberships are available.

Facilities include a driving range, club house, and practice green. The driving range is located on SE McTaggart. At the driving range you can get a bucket of balls for $3-5.

Directions: Take Cherry Lane off Highway 26 and follow the golf course signs.

Prineville

Meadow Lakes Golf Course
9 Holes <> Par 36 <> Length 3131 yards <> $
300 Meadow Lakes Drive - Prineville, OR
541-447-7113
www.meadowlakesgc.com

Built in 1993, Meadow Lakes was designed by William Robinson. This is a links-style course with water on all 18 holes. You also get a nice view of the Ochoco Mountains and the Crooked River. The slope is 131 for men with a rating of 73.1; for women it is 121 and 69.1. The total distance for the ladies' tees is 5155 yards. Open year round, dawn to dusk.

Monday thru Thursday, May thru September, green fees for 9 holes are $18 and $32 for 18. After 1pm they drop to $15 and $25. Juniors pay $10 and $16 all day long. Friday thru Sunday, and on all major holidays, you'll pay

$22 for 9 holes or $38 for 18. After 1pm fees drop to $18 and $28. Juniors play for $12 and $18 on weekends. Rates are lower off season and Tuesdays are cheaper all year; $25 for 18 holes or $20 if you're a senior.

They have a restaurant/lounge with a liquor license, plus a banquet room, snack bar, full-service pro shop, and driving range. The range has grass tees and a bucket of balls is $3.

Directions: Take Highway 26 north and east of Bend.

Redmond

Eagle Crest Resort
54 Holes <> Par 72 <> Length 6927 yards <> $$
1522 Cline Ralls Road - Redmond, OR
541-923-5002 - Reservations Available
www.eagle-crest.com

Eagle Crest has three 18-hole golf courses. The **Ridge Course** is a great place to practice your long shot. On the 3rd hole you'll find a great view of the Cascade Mountains and lots of places to lose your ball. Some water and a couple of good doglegs will keep you on your toes; the slope is 134 and the course rating 72.7. Designed by John Thronson this course opened in 1993. The total distance from the ladies tees is 5616 yards.

The **Resort Course** was designed by Bunny Mason and built in 1986. Its slope is 128 and the ratings 70.8 for a total distance of 6673 yards; from the red tees the length is 5340 yards. This course has three tees for each hole, lots of trees, and a couple of good water hazards. The **Challenge Course** is a par 63, 4160 yard executive course. It's a good place to try for a hole-in-one. The slope is 109 and the course rating 61.1; from the red tees the distance is 2982 yards.

Green fees on the Resort and Ridge Courses are $45 for 9 holes or $69 for 18; off-season rates drop to $35 and $50. In the winter they drop again to $25 and $35. On the Challenge Course you'll pay $44 for 18 holes any time of the year.

Facilities include resort accommodations, fine dining, and a full-service pro shop. They also have a driving range where you can get a bucket of balls for $4.

Directions: Located right in Redmond; look for the signs.

Juniper Golf Club

18 Holes <> Par 72 <> Length 6625 yards <> $$
139 SE Sisters Avenue - Redmond, OR
541-548-3121
www.playjuniper.com

Juniper is open year round, weather permitting. Its original 9 holes were built in 1952 and it was expanded to 18 holes in 1987. The terrain is fairly flat and easy to walk, with four ponds to keep it challenging. The view is impressive and includes several snow-capped mountains.

Juniper's slope is 124 for men and 115 for women. From the ladies' tees the total yardage is 5598. Although this is a semi-private course, they are only closed to the public on Wednesday mornings and Thursday afternoons.

Between the end of May and the middle of September you'll pay $59 for 18 holes on weekdays and $65 on weekends and holidays. Falls brings rates of $30 for 9 holes or $49 for 18; during November 18 holes drops to $39.

Winter green fees are in affect from the end of November until the middle of February; you'll pay $20 and you can play all day.

Facilities include a driving range, pro shop, restaurant and lounge. Lessons are available, and they have a banquet room that holds 180 people for larger tournament gatherings.

Directions: Located east of Highway 97, at the south end of town.

The Greens at Redmond
18 Holes <> Par 58 <> Length 3554 yards <> $$
2475 SW Greens Blvd. - Redmond, OR
541-923-0694

Robert Muir Graves designed this executive curse. It opened in 1995 and has three sets of tees. The 6th hole is a real challenge with both water and a dogleg to overcome for a par four. Open dawn to dusk, year round., the slope is 100 and the course rating 59.0.

Green fees are the same all week long, $20 for 9 holes or $24 for 18. Juniors can play for $10 and $19. Clubs rent for $10, pull carts are $5, and motorized carts $20 for 18 holes.

Facilities include a snack bar serving cold beer and wine, plus a full-service pro shop where you can get help with tournament planning.

Directions: Located right in Redmond and well marked.

Sisters

Aspen Lakes Golf Course
18 Holes <> Par 72 <> Length 7302 yards <> $$
16900 Aspen Lakes Drive – Sisters, OR
541-549-4653
www.aspenlakes.com

The view from Aspen Lakes is outstanding, with the beautiful snow-capped Sisters Mountains and tree-lined fairways. Designed by William Overdorf, this course has multiple tees, red sand bunkers, and bent grass fairways.

Several large ponds and lots of bunkers will challenge your game. The slope is 141 and the course rating 75.4; the women's tees have a total distance of 5594 yards.

Green fees June thru September are $40 for 9 holes or $75 for 18; play before 7am and you pay $45 for 18. October thru late-April green fees are $25 for 9 holes or $45 for 18; play before 7:30am and you'll pay $20 and $35. Sunday evenings after 5pm is Family Night; adults play for $2 a hole and juniors $1 per hole. Pull carts rent for $4 and $6, and motorized carts $12 and $17 per person.

The clubhouse includes a full-service pro shop, café and bar, plus the Brand 33 Restaurant. Facilities include a putting green and a two-level driving range.

Directions: Leave Highway 126 at Camp Polk Road, turn left and go .4 mile to Aspen Lakes Drive. Turn right, the course is on the left.

Sunriver

Sunriver Golf Course
36 Holes <> Par 71 <> Length 7012 yards <> $$$$
Sunriver Resort - Sunriver, OR
541-593-4402 - Reservations Required
www.sunriver-resort.com

Sunriver has three 18-hole golf courses; two are open to the public. The **Meadows Course** borders the Sun River, was designed by John Fought, and has some really nice views.

The slope is 131 and the coursed rating 72.9. You'll find plenty of challenges on this beautiful course with seven holes bordering the river.

The **Woodlands Course** was designed by Robert Trent Jones Jr., has a total distance of 6913 yards, and a par of 72. This course has lots of trees and water, some nice lava rock and great roughs; it was built in 1981.

The slope is 142 and the course rating 73.4. From the ladies tees the total distance is 5341 yards.

Peak season green fees on both the Meadows and Woodlands golf courses are $99 for 18 holes, $69 from 1-5pm, and $49 after 5pm. Juniors pay $40 before 1pm, $35 from 1-5pm, and $30 after 5pm.

From the end of September thru October adults can play all day for $59 and juniors play for $25.

Facilities at Sunriver include a full-service pro shop, banquet facilities, a great restaurant and lounge, deluxe accommodations, and recreational activities. Lessons, and help with tournament planning, are available.

Directions: Located behind Sunriver Lodge.

Tygh Valley

Pine Hollow Golf Course
9 Holes <> Par 34 <> Length 2469 yards <> $
8-A South County Road - Tygh Valley, OR
541-544-2035 - Reservations Available

Pine Hollow's terrain is semi-hilly, and two sets of tees allow you to play 18 holes with variety. The 2nd hole on this course is quite difficult, because of its narrow tree-lined dogleg. Pine Hollow was designed by Earl Davis Jr. and Associates., and opened in 1989. The slope is 95 with a rating of 61.6.

On Tuesday nights the entire course is reserved for men; and on Wednesdays after 10am only the ladies can play. The rest of the week everyone is welcome. The course is open April thru October, dawn to dusk.

Green fees at Pine Hollow are $13 for 9 holes or $20 for 18, all week long. Seniors can play 9 holes for $11 or 18 holes for $18. At times this course is on the honor system, so have the correct change; you'll find a lock box at the clubhouse when no one is on duty.

Facilities include a small pro shop, snack bar, and a putting and chipping area. When the club house is open you can rent clubs and carts.

Directions: Take Highway 197 west of Tygh Valley for 8 miles.

Warm Springs

Kah-Nee-Ta Resort Golf Course
18 Holes <> Par 72 <> Length 6352 yards <> $$
Kah-Nee-Ta Resort - Warm Springs, OR
541-553-1112
www.kahneeta.com

Kah-Nee-Ta is a great place to hide from the rain since it sees sunshine about 300 days out of the year. A year-round course, it has lush greens surrounded by sand and water, large fairways, and a river running alongside. The front 9 was designed by William Bell, the back 9 by Bunny Mason. From the ladies tees the total distance is 5195 yards for par of 73.

Green fees during the spring and summer are $23 for 9 holes or $45 for 18; juniors play for $15 and $25. Seniors, age 55 and older, get a cart on Mondays for the regular non-cart rate. Motorized carts rent for $8 and $16 per rider, and clubs are $10 per 9 holes. Green fees are reduced for resort guests, but anyone can buy an annual pass offering unlimited play.

Facilities included a practice area, full-service pro shop, banquet facilities, and a restaurant and lounge with a liquor license. At the pro shop you can get help with tournament planning and arrange for lessons. The resort offers a luxurious hotel that overlooks the golf course, mineral baths, swimming pool, casino, nearby fishing, horseback riding, tennis, bicycling, and camping.

Directions: Take Highway 26 east toward Warm Springs, turn at the Kah-Nee-Ta junction and go 11 miles.

Region Four

Eastern Oregon

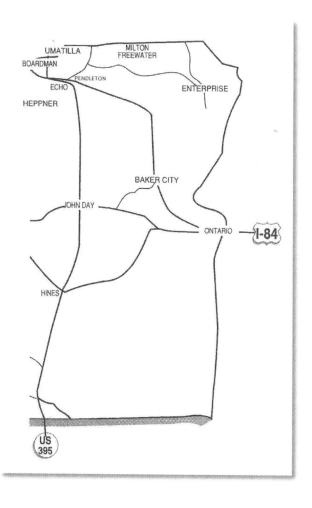

COURSES IN EASTERN OREGON

Eastern Oregon is the state's least populated region, and therefore has the fewest golf courses, only eleven. However, the northwest corner of the state is a gorgeous mountainous terrain, and a popular destination for Oregonians who enjoy history and outdoor recreation, and a game of golf can only add to that fun.

Camping and hiking are popular in the Wallowa Mountains, the eastern edge of the state has lots of good rock hounding areas, and many of the towns were started by Oregon Trail pioneers.

This region's golf courses have sagebrush and tree-filled roughs, natural canyons and gullies, natural creeks and rivers, and high desert altitudes that will challenge your endurance.

The following cities in Eastern Oregon have golf courses.

Baker City
Boardman
Echo
Enterprise
Heppner
Hines

John Day
Milton-Freewater
Ontario
Pendleton
Umatilla

Baker City

Quail Ridge Golf Course
18 Holes <> Par 72 <> Length 5975 yards <> $
2810 Indiana Avenue - Baker City, OR
541-523-2358
www.quailridgegreens.com

Quail Ridge is flat with relatively few obstacles; a creek comes into play on three holes and the surroundings are pleasant, with Elk Horn and the Eagle Mountains in the background. Designed by Bill Robinson, and built in 1936, this course is open April thru November.

The 7th hole drops 20 vertical feet as it travels over a small water hazard, the 10th takes you across a deep gully, and the 11th, when played right, can result in a birdie. Occasionally closed for tournaments, you'll want to call ahead during peak season. The white tees have a total distance of 5697 yards, the red ones 5035; the women's par is 70 and the course slope is 118 to 121.

Green fees are $17 for 9 holes or $25 for 18 all week long. During the week, when the course is not too busy, golfers 14 and younger can play for $13 and $18, and kids 13 and younger can play with an adult golfer for free. Everyone can take advantage of the bargain rates that start at 4pm Friday thru Wednesday; the cost is $12.50 whether you play 9 or 18 holes. When Taco Tuesdays are in season you can play 9 or 18 for $12.50 any time of the day.

Facilities include a public lounge with a liquor license, a BBQ shack, plus banquet facilities, and a full service pro shop where you can get help with tournament planning and lessons.

Directions: Take Highway 7 out of Baker City and follow the signs; it's just 1 mile from the center of town.

Boardman

Wilson's Willow Run Golf
9 Holes <> Par 31 <> Length 1803 yards <> $
78873 Toms Camp Road - Boardman, OR
541-481-4381

Willow Run is an interesting course with lots of water. Open March thru November, the course is closed on Mondays, unless it is a holiday weekend. This course opened in 1972 and was designed by Dallas Wilson. It is easy to walk but sometimes can be windy. The slope is 88 and the course rating 59; it takes about 1.5 hours to play 9 holes.

Facilities include a small pro shop where you'll find snacks and cold drinks, plus a clubhouse. During the week green fees are $12 for 9 holes and $18 for 18 holes; on weekends and holidays you'll pay $15 and $20. High school students can purchase an annual pass that lets them play for reduced rates. Rental equipment is available; they rent clubs, handcarts and motorized carts.

Directions: Wilson's Willow Run Golf Course is located 4 miles southwest of Boardman on Wilson Road.

Echo

Echo Hills Golf Course
9 Holes <> Par 36 <> Length 2884 yards <> $
400 Golf Course Road - Echo, OR
541-376-8244 - Reservations Advised
www.echo-oregon.com

On a clear day you can see both Mt. Adams and Rainier from the Echo Hills course. Opened in 1933, the terrain is hilly with sagebrush-filled roughs and trees separating the fairways. Open year round, the slope is 117 and the course rating 34.4. The middle tees have a par of 37, a slope of 113, and a distance of 2607 yards.

On weekends and holidays you can play 9 holes for $14 or 18 for $23. Weekday green fees are $12 and $20, but juniors get to play for $7 and $14. Punch cards let students play 10 rounds for $50 on weekdays and after 4pm on weekends; adults can purchase 20-round punch cards for weekday play for $200. They offer rental clubs, handcarts, and motorized carts; if you bring your own motorized cart the trail fee is $8.

Facilities include a driving range, pro shop, and a snack bar that serves beer and wine. Assistance with tournament planning is available. The driving range offers both mat and grass tees.

Directions: Located 1 mile off I-84 by way of exit #188. After heading south, turn left at the school and left again 4 blocks later. From there follow the signs to Echo Hills.

Enterprise

Alpine Meadows Golf Course
9 Holes <> Par 36 <> Length 3033 yards <> $$
66098 Golf Course Road - Enterprise, OR
541-426-3246
www.alpinemeadowsgolfcourse.com

Open April thru October, reservations are not needed at Alpine Meadows. The terrain is flat and easy to walk and they offer two sets of tees. This is a beautiful course with a brook running across the fairways and a panoramic view of the Wallowa Mountains. It was built in the 1930's, sits 3756' above sea level, and is surrounded by low rolling hills. The course rating is 35 and the slope 116.

Green fees are $20 for 9 holes or $32 for 18 all week long. Juniors and seniors can buy annual passes for discounted play. Clubs rent for $8-13, handcarts are $4-6, and motorized carts $15-28. If you bring your own motorized cart the trail fee is $20.

Facilities include a putting green, chipping green, small pro shop, and banquet facilities. The snack shack has drinks and snacks, including beer, wine and mixed drinks. You'll find it in the clubhouse, which is open from 7am to 8pm. Lessons, and help with tournament planning, are available.

Directions: Located near the west end of town.

Heppner

Willow Creek Country Club
9 Holes <> Par 30 <> Length 1725 yards <> $
53726 Hwy. 74 - Heppner, OR
541-676-5437

This year-round course opened in 1954, has a gently rolling terrain, and narrow fairways. A creek comes into play on five holes. Willow Creek began with just 1 hole, gradually grew to 3, and then expanded into a full 9-hole course. The course rating is 58.2 and the slope 82; two sets of tees provide variety for 18-hole play.

Fees are a real bargain at Willow Creek; 9 holes are $12 and 18 holes $20 all week long, or you can play all day for $25. Cart and club rental is available. They have a limited pro shop, open March thru October, where you'll find help with tournament planning.

Directions: Located 1 mile north of Heppner, on Highway 74.

Hines

Valley Golf Club
9 Holes <> Par 36 <> Length 3190 yards <> $
345 Hines Blvd. - Hines, OR
541-573-6251 - Reservations Advised

Valley Golf is open year round, weather permitting. The course is flat and easy to walk. First opened in 1939, it was designed by Shelby McCool. Two sets of tees are available; the fairways are winter rye and the greens bent grass. The forward tees have a total distance of 2747 yards; the slope is 107, and the course rating 34.7. The middle tees are 3190 yards, the slope is 117, and the rating 36.6.

Green fees remain the same all week long at this reversible 9-hole course. You'll pay $15 for 9 holes or $25 for 18. Clubs can be rented for $2 and handcarts are

$1. Gas carts are $10 for 9 holes or $18 for 18. Lessons are available, ask at the pro shop.

Directions: Located on Highway 20, in Hines.

John Day

John Day Golf Club
9 Holes <> Par 35 <> Length 2930 yards <> $
27631 Golf Club Lane - John Day, OR
541-575-0170 - Reservations Advised

The John Day Golf Course is open year round, except when snow prevents play. Located 3200' above sea level, this hilly course offers a beautiful view of Rudio Canyon and the Blue Mountains. This is a semi-private course, and can be closed for tournaments, so call ahead.

The fairways are tree lined and the greens small. This course has a rating of 33.6 and a slope of 111. On the 4th hole you have to shoot over the lake; on the 7th hole you have to avoid the lake. Two sets of tees are available; the second set has a total distance of 2854 yards and a course rating of 35.6. This semi-private course first opened in 1953.

All week long green fees are $12 for 9 holes or $22 for 18. You can rent clubs for $5, handcarts $2, and motorized carts are $10 for 9 holes or $20 for 18. Hours are 10am Monday thru Friday, they open at 9am on weekends, and they always close at dusk.

They have a putting green, chipping area, snack bar with alcohol, and a limited pro shop where you can get help with tournament planning. It opens at 8am, and they have a driving range with grass tees where you'll pay $2 for a bucket of balls.

Directions: Located 3 miles west of John Day on Highway 26.

Milton-Freewater

Milton-Freewater Golf Course
18 Holes <> Par 60 <> Length 3346 yards <> $$
301 Catherine Street - Milton-Freewater
541-938-7284 - Reservations Advised
www.mfcity.com/golfcourse

This executive course offers a flat bottom nine and a hilly upper nine; there is a 125' difference in elevation. From the upper nine you have a fabulous view of the Walla Walla Valley and the Blue Mountains. The slope is 80 and the course rating 55.4.

Open 362 days a year, weather permitting. The first nine holes were built in 1973 and the second opened in 1986. The women's tees have a par of 61 for a total distance of

3314 yards. After the game relax at Shelly's Last Shot Restaurant over good food and your favorite beverage.

March thru October green fees are $16 for 9 holes or $24 for 18, seven days a week. Seniors and students play for $11 and $17. Monthly passes and 12-game punch cards bring those prices down even more. Off-season rates are slashed in half.

Directions: This course is located right in Milton-Freewater; the route is well marked.

Ontario

Country View Golf Course
9 Holes <> Par 36 <> Length 2830 yards <> $
3780 Arabian Drive - Ontario, OR
541-881-1171
www.cvgc.us

This course has lots of steep hills, a few good blind shots, and good short greens; it's a fun little course. Once an 80-acre farm, you'll find tree-lined fairways and sagebrush in the roughs. Wildlife is often seen on the course; the slope varies from 105-121 depending on which tees you use. The course opened in 1999 and was designed by Scott McKinney.

Green fees are $14 for 9 holes or $20 for 18. College students play for $10 and $16; juniors and high school students play for $8 and $14. Rental clubs are $5, pull carts $2, and motorized carts $6-12 per person.

There is a driving range; you can get a bucket of range balls for $4-5. Facilities include a pro shop and a full snack bar.

Directions: Located 8 miles out of town. Leave US 20 on Onion Avenue and turn right on Arabian Drive. Follow this to the course.

Shadow Butte Golf Course
18 Holes <> Par 71 <> Length 6670 yards <> $$
1345 Golf Course Road - Ontario, OR
541-889-9022

The Shadow Butte Golf Course is situated in the shadow of Malheur Butte. It opened in 1965, designed by Bob Baldock, and was once the longest course in the state. You'll find excellent greens, very few hills, and a terrain that is easy to walk. The slope is 115 and the course rating 69.4. Shadow Butte is open February 15th thru the end of November.

Green fees are $18 for 9 holes or $33 for 18, all week long. Facilities include a snack bar, a restaurant with a liquor license, plus a driving range and pro shop. Lessons are available.

Directions: Located 1 mile west on Highway 201.

THE NORTHWEST GOLFER: OREGON EDITION

Pendleton

Wildhorse Resort Golf Course
18 Holes <> Par 72 <> Length 7128 yards <> $$
46510 Wildhorse Blvd. - Pendleton, OR
541-276-5588 - Reservations Available

The Wildhorse Casino course opened in 1997 and was designed by John Steidel. It offers spectacular views, blue grass fairways, and bent grass greens. You'll find lots of water, plenty of sand, a couple of doglegs, and lots of trees. Four sets of tees make this semi-private course fun yet challenging for all levels of players; the total distance from the ladies' tees is 5718 yards. Open year round, the course rating is 73.8 and the slope 125.

Green fees Monday thru Thursday are $16 for 9 holes or $28 for 18. Friday thru Sunday you'll pay $19 and $34. On Tuesdays and Thursdays seniors, age 60 and older, play for $20; juniors, age 16 and younger, play for half price daily after 1pm. Power carts add $8.50 and $13 per player.

Facilities include a restaurant and lounge, casino, resort accommodations, full-service pro shop, putting and practice greens, a driving range, and a RV park. At the driving range you can get a bucket of balls for $4-8, depending on how many you need.

Directions: Leave I-84 at exit #216 and follow the casino signs; located 6.7 miles east of Pendleton.

Umatilla

Big River Golf Course
18 Holes <> Par 70 <> Length 5975 yards <> $
709 Willamette - Umatilla, OR
541-922-3006 - Reservations Advised
www.golfbigriver.com

This moderately flat course was built in the 1940s and is open year round. It has a view of the Columbia River and operates from daylight to dark. And although this may look like an easy course, it's not. The greens are good and the roughs natural. Par from the ladies' tees is 74 for a distance of 5940 yards.

Weekday green fees are $13 for 9 holes or $25 for 18. On weekends and holidays they charge $14 and $27. Juniors play for $11 and $17. Pull carts rent for $10 and $18; motorized carts are $10 and $18 for a single golfer or $13 and $15 for more players. The trail fee when you bring your own cart is $6 and $10.

Winter rates are $10 for 9 holes no matter who plays; for 18 holes juniors pay $17 and everyone else pays $20. Power carts are $5 and $10 for a single golfer, $10 and $20 for more players.

Directions: Located 1 mile east of town, right off Highway 730, in McNary Addition.

INDEX

The Northwest Golfer
Twenty-fifth Anniversary Edition

The *Northwest Golfer* by KiKi Canniff provides Oregon and Washington golfers with a quick way to find every public golf course in each state.

This 25th Anniversary Edition is available in both print and eBook formats, giving golfers two ways to keep the region's more than 350 public golf courses handy. This is the first eBook release of the book; the print version made its first debut in 1987.

The Northwest Golfer is laid out directory-style, making it easy to find all nearby courses quickly. The Amazon Kindle eBook version is interactive, and includes links to course websites, making it essential for the avid golfer's phone or laptop.

Each listing begins with a handy reference line revealing the course's yardage, par, the number of holes and price range, giving golfers quick access to important details. This is followed by full contact information, including websites when available. Information on the course's terrain, designer, history, facilities, scenic beauty, current green fees, equipment rental rates, and when you can play for less are all covered within each listing.

With this edition, each state has its own volume. *The Northwest Golfer - Washington Edition* contains complete details on that state's 201 public and semi-private golf course sites; multiple courses at some sites give the state 218 public courses in all. *The Northwest Golfer - Oregon Edition* provides full details on the 144 course locations in Oregon; some of these sites also sport multiple courses.

This is not an armchair-style guide; there are no photographs or illustrations. But, if you play golf in Oregon or Washington it puts all of the important details at your fingertips, allowing you to find every public course quickly.

Made in the USA
Lexington, KY
10 June 2015